To Bill —

Arlene
+
Ron

First edition

Born Stateless

State-less (*state-lis)* Adjective - having no state or nationality

A Young Man's Story 1923 to 1957

Kon Balin as told to Arlene Balin

authorHOUSE®

AuthorHouse™
1663 Liberty Drive
Bloomington, IN 47403
www.authorhouse.com
Phone: 1-800-839-8640

First published by AuthorHouse 9/25/2009

ISBN: 978-1-4490-0680-8 (e)
ISBN: 978-1-4490-0658-7 (sc)

Library of Congress Control Number: 2009907159

Printed in the United States of America
Bloomington, Indiana

This book is printed on acid-free paper.

To my wife, Arlene, whose insistence and endurance, translated "stubbornness", resulted in this book being completed.

✐✐

THANKS TO:

Ms. Wendy Lichtman who suggested, praised and cri-
tiqued this memoir with kindness and patience.
Ms. Anna Detrick who helped prepare text
and photos for publication and
offered wonderful suggestions and insights.
All of the brave souls who read the first drafts of our
book and gave us the impetus to continue.

◈

TABLE OF CONTENTS

Thanks to: vii

Forward xi

The Beginning of My Story 1

The Bolshevik Revolution 1917—1921—Khabarovsk,

Siberia 4

Harbin, What To Do Now 9

Childhood—Growing Up Being Different {Gaijin} 13

Where We Lived and How We Lived 16

The First Big Change 26

Our Own Home 29

Our Education 32

Second Big Change 44

My Senior Year and Beyond 47

Shanghai, the Paris of the Far East 51

Shanghai, 1941 58

My Life as a Student Goes On 64

The Victorious Japanese—1942 66

Entering St. John's University and a Visit Home 68

Living with Nobility 72

Curfews and Lonely Soldiers 80

Everything Gets Worse 89

Sven, The Policeman 98

Stealing to Survive 101

The Japanese and the Jewish People 103

Planes Above Us 105

The War is Over 108

Soviet Solictation 132

Boris 134

The Allies Arrive in Shanghai 138

Auxiliary Military Police.. 143

A New Job In Peking... 147

Peking, the Ancient City 152

Back in Shanghai.. 160

Return to Japan—1947.. 162

My Family's Survival Journey 165

General MacArthur and the Birth of a New Japan 169

The Need for Entertainment 171

1948—Learning the Import/Export Business 176

Family Life Returns.. 179

Fun Begins 182

My Own Business... 187

And Then There Was One 192

Searching for Undesirables... 196

And Then There Was One – Continued.......................... 199

The Story of Ronald Kirkbride and the Story He Told ..206

Yoshi 208

And it Began 210

Back to Work and a Bit of Play 214

In the Meantime.. 219

Epilogue 225

FORWARD

Kon Balin has been my friend for over forty years and my husband for thirteen. He is a good looking, charming and sophisticated man with a slight foreign accent, who does not in any way look or act like a man eighty-six years old.

At every cocktail or dinner party someone inevitably asks him where he was born. "I am Chinese" he says with a smile and waits for the questioner's "ha ha".

"But it's true." And Kon goes on to explain. "My father was a Russian cavalry officer fighting the Bolsheviks in Siberia. My parents had to flee into Manchuria after the revolution. I was born in Harbin, China. When I was two the family moved to Japan and I was raised there. My schooling was provided by American Catholic brothers so I grew up in three languages."

I usually excuse myself from these conversations, but I enjoy watching the interest and rapt attention that ensues as Kon tells his stories and answers their questions. Many times men will hand him their name cards and ask Kon to call them for lunch to hear more about his unusual life. Women are equally fascinated with the man I married and love being his dinner partner. The conversations invariably end with "You should write a book."

It took a long time to convince him to let me write down his remembrances. It has taken over four years to complete this little book.

The image I have of Kon Balin is that of a stately old house with ageless character and style. The façade is well cared for, the brass door knocker is burnished from years of polishing. When I walk into this house the public rooms are what one would expect, but upon reaching the top of the stairway and opening the doors of the rooms, I see layers of dust and cobwebs in the musty corners. Some of the doors are impossible to open, locked by some long lost key.

As we worked on each story and opened the door on those dusty memories it was evident that Kon did not want to go any deeper than the entertaining anecdotes he had told for years. If I asked him what someone looked like or how he felt about a situation he would be annoyed and accuse me of interrupting. Finally, I came across a way we could relate the stories of his young life. "Just tell me the story and I will take notes and write the chapter, then you can correct it." That seemed to work. With each rewrite more was revealed. The rooms filled with dust and cobwebs were aired if not always swept entirely clean. People, places and feelings that were hidden under old sheets were uncovered revealing treasures from another age. Some rooms stayed locked, perhaps never to be opened.

As you read these tales about Kon as a young man living in Japan and Shanghai during the 1920s to the 1950s, I hope you will get a sense of what it was like for that boy who was born stateless, uncertain whether he would live or die and never really belonging anywhere. For those who are friends and family, I hope you will have a deeper understanding of the man born Konstantin Policarpovich Balabushkin and became Kon Balin. His survival in the tragic and often inhuman times in which he lived took its toll, but he endured. Despite his successes, sorrows and some shame perseveres, trying always to be a better man. It is not in his nature to give up.

∽∾

THE BEGINNING OF MY STORY

The stroke of a stranger's pen in late December, 1956 marked the end of my life in Japan. When I began the process of remembering the bits and pieces of my life as a young man I realized something I suppose most old people discover. Anyone who believes he or she is in control and creates the path on which one starts his or her life is at best naïve and at worst, a fool.

It is not difficult to understand why analogies often refer to roads when describing one's life's journey. The bumps in the road, the detours, the warning signs alerting one to dangerous curves and slippery slopes all fit nicely, don't they? But, for each of us that road begins through no plan of our making. Every experience, every person we meet leaves an imprint. Whether one believes in God, providence or fate, we all begin our unique journey on a specific road already set in place. My journey began where it did because of a revolution that took place before I was born.

෴

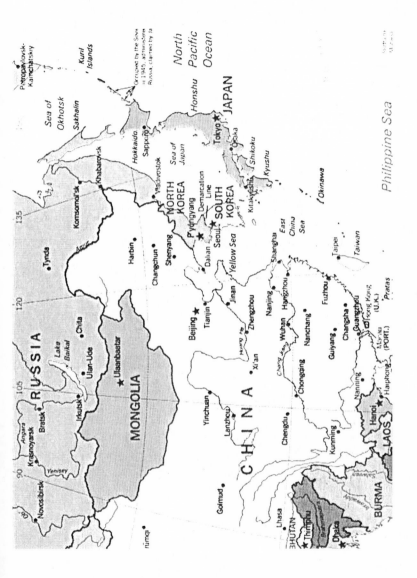

3

THE BOLSHEVIK REVOLUTION 1917—1921—KHABAROVSK, SIBERIA

During the Siberian campaign in the early 1920s my father's regiment was quartered in one of the larger cities in Siberia named Khabarovsk, waiting for supplies and reorganizing in order to continue fighting for the Tsar and Imperial Russia. I don't know how my father met my mother, but I do know it was in this city that they found each other. My mother was a tall, slim girl from a well-to-do merchant family, the oldest of three children with a younger sister and brother. She attended private schools where she wore mandatory, ladylike uniforms as evidenced from old photographs that somehow were saved. My father's family was part of the landed gentry in the Ukraine, or so I have been told. He had five sisters and two brothers. The older brother was a colonel in the army and the younger was an officer in the navy. My father was a captain in the cavalry and from his pictures he appears handsome and quite a cavalier. They were married within a year.

My parent's chance meeting in Khabarovsk changed their lives forever and caused mine to begin. Pictures in books depicting Russian men with long beards sitting next to women in heavily embroidered dresses and headpieces in no way resembled my parents, but in many ways they were part of that world. Perhaps, in the complicated realm of gene memory I too am part of that long gone era.

The Russian Revolution of 1917 lasted almost four years. Lenin had fled to Europe because of his Marxist beliefs and actions that provoked the masses, putting his life in danger. He was able to clandestinely return to Russia after the 1917 October Russian Navy Revolt in St. Petersburg. It was the right time for Lenin to return. The First World War, which began with an outpouring of love and support for the weakened Tsar, ended up a disaster for the Russian people both economically and politically, exacerbating the grave unrest of the populace. There were many who wanted a parliamentary type government, but the Bolsheviks were too well organized and lead by a totally focused Lenin. Harsh fighting in the streets and riots ensued. Finally, many in the military turned toward the Reds and on October 25, 1917 the naval crew of the ship "Aurora" shot blanks at the Winter Palace. That first gunshot from the "Aurora" has come to be known as "The shot heard round the world", and the October Russian Navy Revolt really began the Revolution.

While the Reds had initial success in central Russia, the Tsarists (Whites) started regrouping in areas like southern Russia, Ukraine and Siberia. Because of the vastness of Russia, all these areas were mostly untouched by the Reds. The Whites, after reorganizing, actually started advancing toward Moscow. But due to poor communications, coordination and indecision, not to mention the bickering among the far flung Whites, the Reds were able to repel their attacks and eventually got control of most of European Russia. The only meaningful resistance left was the White army in Siberia, where the Reds were starting to press eastward from the Ural Mountains. That is where my father's regiment was, the last stand of the weakened Russian army that had all but exhausted every hope of winning the war.

The Whites suffered innumerable hardships. Most importantly, they lacked the equipment necessary to fight a war successfully. For example, crossing the frozen Baikal Lake in winter was extremely perilous. Baikal is the largest fresh water lake in the world. It has a long, narrow, north to south shape. During the mild summers the trains ran on tracks going around the lake, but in the harsh winters, with temperatures below zero, the tracks were laid on the frozen surface of the lake. It was while crossing this frozen lake that my father told me he had to shoot his horse because it lacked the necessary spiked shoes that prevented his beloved mount from sliding on the treacherous ice.

Despite the perseverance of the White army who bravely tried to hold on, the Reds, with help from some European nations who did not want a powerful Russian Empire, started pushing the White Army eastward.

The Reds prevailed and concluded the brutal and bloody revolution by killing many White leaders, both military and civilian. The Tsar had already abdicated and was living with his family in a retreat located in the Ural Mountains in a city called Ekaterinburg. The Tsar and his whole family were executed in the middle of the night by the Bolsheviks who were afraid the Tsar's loyal followers would start a counter-revolution.

Both of my father's brothers were captured by the Reds and executed. His older brother was shot, and the younger brother, after having his arms wrenched out of their sockets, was thrown into the sea as was the custom for naval execution.

Meanwhile, thousands of White Russians, both military and civilian, who had reached far eastern Siberia, were trying to escape the advancing Reds. A large number fled to Harbin, a city located in the northern Chinese province of Manchuria bordering Siberia. They crossed the Amur River, which separated Manchuria and Siberia. Harbin had a large Russian population even before the Revolution. In the late 1800's, Russia had built a railroad from Siberia to Harbin, a distance of about 250 miles (325 kilometers). The railroad was serviced and manned by Russians in Manchuria. Quite a few White Russian refugees made their way from Harbin to places like Shanghai and Tientsin, China.

When the revolution finally ended in disaster, my parents were forced to flee, as did many other anti-communist Russians. They took separate routes out of Siberia into Manchuria. The railway in Manchuria was still managed and operated by the Whites. My mother boarded the train to Harbin, leaving her home, family and all she had known since childhood. I have often thought that my mother's character and determination were first tested at this time. They were to be tested many times in the next two decades.

Because the railroads in Siberia were being watched by the Communists in order to thwart the escape routes of the Whites, especially military men, a different and safer path had to be taken by my father. Somehow he made it on foot to the Amur River, crossed it, and eventually was able to reach Harbin where my mother was waiting along with thousands of other Russian refugees. Not only did the White Russians lose the war, they lost their country and had become stateless.

؇؇

HARBIN, WHAT TO DO NOW

In the early 1920's, in the aftermath of the Revolution, Harbin was a city teaming with travelers and refugees, all hoping to escape tyranny and violence. White Russians, Jews, Tatars, and many other displaced peoples huddled in Harbin trying to survive. My parents were just two people like all the others.

Having been trained and educated as a military man, my father had no skills to market except his knowledge of horses. He found employment as a "hackey", a driver of a horse drawn carriage, still the most popular form of city transportation. Motorized taxis were just starting to be seen on the streets of Harbin. Life was very difficult, but my father was able to eke out a living. Despite the hardships they were forced to endure, I was born on June 24th, 1923 and my sister, Ludmila, nicknamed Lala, was born in August of 1925.

My father was a very proud man. To be caught in a downward spiral of happenstance which resulted in the destruction of all he respected must have caused grave emotional anguish resulting in bouts of angry depression. That deep-seated anger emerged in explosions of rage and continued at times throughout his life. Humiliation, poverty, desperation and the constant pressure of not having control of his destiny were now part of his life day in and day out.

My mother was also thrust into a world she never could have imagined, but she remained calm, even unflappable. Well educated, secure in her place on the social scale of early 20th century Russia, she had been like every other pretty girl who married a handsome officer. She had reason to believe all would work out. It did not. She adjusted. One of my mother's greatest assets was her ability to read situations, sensing when to speak and when to remain silent. It is difficult to understand the love (or lack of it) between one's parents. I suppose when there is deep and genuine love all is understood and eventually forgiven. My mother was able to cope and probably my father was able to go on because my mother continued to love and encourage him during this hard time in Harbin.

Optimism and courage were qualities both my parents embraced. They still hoped for a better future. That hope was about to become a reality.

During those unsettled and chaotic times it was common for people to seek information about lost family members and friends from people they met coming and going from one place to another. It was in this way that my father's young military aide, a Tatar named Kamkin, heard of my father's whereabouts. Tatars were Muslim people from southern Russia loyal to the Tsar. For some unknown reason, Kamkin, in the frantic confusion leaving Siberia, landed in Japan instead of Manchuria. Like many Tatars who were experts in the weaving of rugs, he had a working knowledge of woolen textiles.

The Japanese were rapidly westernizing their manner of dress. Men wanted to wear suits and coats to their workplace instead of kimonos. Women also were beginning to want modern, western attire. Those foreigners, who could help with this transition, were respected and sought after. Although Kamkin was young, he was enterprising and soon had developed a successful business in the woolens trade. When he learned of his captain's hard times in Harbin, he wrote my father, and offered to teach him what he knew. "Come to Japan", he wrote. And so it was that my father, grasping at any opportunity to provide for his family, journeyed to Japan. He left my mother with whatever money he had for our sustenance.

Although she had friends, she was alone caring for her two small children. But being resolute she went on. I never remember my mother complaining about anything throughout her life. My parents wrote to each other often, my father sending as much money as he could. It was about six months before the letter finally arrived telling my mother to join him in Japan and with the necessary funds to make the trip. My father, with the help of Kamkin, learned the basics of the woolen business and was confident he could achieve more in Japan than Harbin. With my baby sister in her arms and me, a two year old, toddling beside her, we left Harbin, first by train to Pusan, the most southern port in Korea, then by boat to Nagasaki, a southern port in Kyushu, Japan, and then by train again, eventually reaching the capital of Japan, the beautiful city of Tokyo. Another new beginning! The year was 1925.

CHILDHOOD—GROWING UP BEING DIFFERENT {GAIJIN}

From my earliest memories, my sister and I had an amah, a children's caretaker. My mother was kept busy managing our home, doing the planning and shopping for meals, cooking, sewing, seeing that the laundry was done and all the other traditional duties of a housewife. But she had to accomplish all these tasks with no knowledge of the language or customs of her new surroundings.

We called our amah "Obachan", a very affectionate title similar to Grandma. In those days older women were traditionally the responsibility of their sons. If a Japanese woman was not fortunate to bear a son, she sometimes found herself in need of employment in her later years. The position of amah was greatly prized.

Our amah was a small woman with black hair streaked with grey and pulled away from her face in a neat bun. She always wore a kimono on her slender frame. In what I later realized, my sister and I were treated like all other Japanese children by our amah. She lived with us and played with us. There was no hugging or kissing and yet we felt loved and perhaps more importantly, liked by that dear woman. I remember her soft voice and gentle ways. As she read to us she showed us pictures and encouraged us to say words in her language. We drew pictures and she would praise us and urge us to tell her in Japanese what we had drawn such as a picture of a house or a tree. First we learned the names of things and then those words would be put into simple conversation. It was like learning a new game. Because we were so young, my sister and I learned Japanese along with Russian. There was a time that we spoke better Japanese than Russian much to the consternation of our parents. The same patience and kindness was shown as we were taught how to eat with "hashi" (chopsticks) and sit properly while we ate. Discipline was firm, but never with a hint of humiliation.

When the sky was clear we were taken on walks. As we passed Japanese women they could not resist stopping us to touch our hair which was quite blond at the time. The ladies would say, "like corn silk". This must have happened many times because my recollection is so clear that I can still remember their soft touch on my head. As I grew older I yearned to have black hair and slanted dark eyes like everyone else. Once in a while when we were on our walks Japanese children would shout after us "Gaijin" meaning foreigner.

Feelings of being different were part of our daily experience. Sometimes I think those feelings have never left me. No one was cruel to me or my sister, but our neighbors made it clear that we were not part of their world. Gaijin. Foreigner. Outsider. Not Japanese. You may wonder how a child reacts to those unspoken messages. I became aggressive by instinct rather than by ever hearing the old saying, "the best defense is a strong offense". In my own quiet way I became a boy to be reckoned with. I found that I was respected for my bravado. I remember feeling shy and sometimes even afraid on the inside, but on the outside my survival skills emerged with laughter and toughness. I became a leader and enjoyed it immensely. It helped being much taller than the Japanese boys my age.

As "curiosities", sometimes to our great annoyance, we would be stopped by total strangers wanting to talk to us, asking all kinds of questions. They were inquisitive without being impolite. Many a time people would ask us where we lived and if they could meet our mother. Later, after they met my mother, some of these nice people took us to the park and even to department stores to buy us treats. We would be royally treated and entertained usually arriving home with presents. Japanese people love children and they are a very curious people. There does not seem any other reason for their attention.

Later on when we began playing with these same Japanese children, who were now our friends, we joined them in shouting "gaijin" when a westerner walked by. We wanted so desperately to fit in and eventually we thought we did.

❧

WHERE WE LIVED AND HOW WE LIVED

Japan in the late 1920's and early 30's was a country of contrasts. Modern ways were combined with ancient Samurai customs imbedded in the culture and philosophy of its people. The central part of Tokyo was a mirror of western progress, but the outlying neighborhoods, where we and other families lived, remained very traditional. The small Japanese style house that we rented was located on a narrow side street. There were many houses on both sides of our unpaved street, no two alike. They were constructed of wood with tile roofs. Most homes had small, well kept gardens in the back. Although the Japanese people prized personal cleanliness, the public areas at that time were less than pristine with paper and other small bits of trash left in the street. Our neighbors were all Japanese. Everyone was friendly, but with a formality common to the country and the times.

Our house was of typical Japanese design, perhaps a bit larger than most. Upon entering the front sliding doors, there was a square foyer with a platform for shoes and slippers. The wooden floors were raised about two feet and covered with "tatami", straw mats roughly three by six feet and about two and a half inches thick. Rooms were measured by these mat sizes. Two tatamis would be a room roughly six by six feet in size; three tatamis would be about six by nine and so on. Once you exchanged your outdoor shoes for indoor slippers, you stepped up one or two stairs to the living quarters. A small landing was crossed to enter the sitting room closed off by "shoji" (wood framed rice paper screened sliding doors). Smaller Japanese houses did not have hallways or corridors on the inside of the house, the rooms separated by "shojis". Rooms facing the outside usually had glass sliding doors. On the other side of these glass doors were wooden doors that were closed at night and in inclement weather. Sliding glass windows were used extensively to let in light. Japanese houses farther from the city center had very basic electrical services.

To the right of the sitting room were two bedrooms and a very small room for our amah. There were Japanese style closets, usually one "tatami" size, with a full shelf at mid height. This is where the Japanese stored their neatly folded clothes and "futons" (bedding). Attire like coats and hats were hung outside the closets on hooks or pegs. The bath room held an oval wooden tub, about three by four feet and three feet high. It was filled with water from a spout. The water was heated by a coal stove built into the side of the tub. The floor was made of wood slats and raised, making it easy to enter into the high tub. When one began the bathing ritual, one would sit or squat on the wood floor, wash with soap and rinse off with clean water scooped from a small, separate compartment of the tub. The water would go through the slatted floor to a drain beneath. After one was completely clean, only then did one enter the hot, soothing water in the tub for a relaxing soak. We performed this ritual at least twice a week.

The toilet room consisted of a porcelain pot placed low on the floor that one had to squat over to use. In the ground under the toilet was a large earthenware container. The contents of these containers were emptied on a regular basis by "honey bucket" collectors. Except in central parts of Tokyo, very few places had flush toilets.

To the left of the dining room was a kitchen, small and primitive by today's standards. There was cold, running water from a faucet and nearby was a gas burner on which was possibly the first portable oven. The oven consisted of a metal box placed on top of the gas burner. Many delicious meals and desserts were made in that oven such as "Kulich", a sweet bread traditionally served at Easter. We had no place to keep perishables, not even an icebox, requiring my mother to shop daily for food.

In each neighborhood there was cluster of shops that met the needs of the families residing nearby. Although the main streets in our neighborhood were paved, there were many narrow lanes, like the one on which we lived. They were of packed dirt with stone pavers on which to walk in rainy weather. Very few people owned automobiles, including our family. We all walked, cycled or took the many convenient trains and buses wherever we wanted to go.

The everyday mode of dress for the ordinary housewife living in the outskirts of downtown Tokyo was still the traditional kimono. Men who wore western style garb to work, quickly changed to kimonos when they arrived home. The kimono is actually a very simple and practical garment. Most of us have seen pictures of Geishas wearing the extravagantly embroidered robes with obis of the finest silk brocade. Those formal kimonos were not the everyday dress of average Japanese people. Their kimonos were made of cotton cloth that came in bolts of about fifteen inches in width. Traditionally the kimono was stitched by hand and even after the invention of the sewing machine the kimono was hand sewn. To wash the kimono the housewife would undo all the seams, wash the fabric by hand, hang it on the clothesline, stretch the material so it would dry unwrinkled and then sew it back together. Kimonos fit almost any body type and allowed the wearer to sit comfortably on tatamis, while dining and conversing. With no western style toilets, the kimono was very practical indeed.

As one ventured into the center of the city, the home of the Emperor, there was a dramatic difference. The streets were all paved, the wide ones having sidewalks. Newer structures were built in contemporary architectural styles. Fashionable shops featured modern clothes and accessories from the west. Elegant office buildings, hotels, theaters and restaurants were starting to be integrated into the sleek city blocks. Parked in front of these establishments one would see expensive automobiles with chauffeurs waiting for their owners to finish their business in town.

Our family was not part of this glittering, sophisticated world. Our social and, of course, religious life, revolved around the Russian Orthodox Church in the center of the city, built in an elegant, Byzantine design. There was no specific area in Tokyo where Russian immigrant families lived. Several hundred of us were scattered all over the city. Most traveled by train or bus every Sunday to worship at the only onion-domed Orthodox Church in Tokyo. Here the families shared news and gossip in a language they all knew. The service was very long, sometimes two or more hours and the congregation stood throughout the service. There were no pews, and it was not unusual for a person to leave for a while in order to rest and then return later.

After church my parents visited with friends and we played with the other children. Then we went for our Sunday treat. We went to lunch and to the movies!

The movie theater near the Russian church was not a theater at all. It was more like a meeting hall with a modest stage over which hung a small motion picture screen. The seating was not conducive to comfort. Everyone sat on backless benches with no cushions. To the side of the screen, in a darkened corner, was a piano being played by a hidden Japanese man who created all manner of sound effects. The piano player adjusted his tempo to fit the flickering black and white images on the screen. He also translated the mostly English subtitles into Japanese, imitating appropriate female and male voices. This talented man in the shadows set the mood. The audience, adults and children alike, were transported from that makeshift movie house to the western plains of America where cowboys and Indians fought gory battles riding spirited horses. We entered the drawing rooms of the very wealthy, glamorous people sipping drinks from cocktail glasses and we cheered as the swashbucklers swung on ropes while they saved the ship from evil pirates!

There were usually two features, one foreign and one Japanese. We saw Charlie Chaplin, Mary Pickford, Douglas Fairbanks, Tom Mix and all the big American screen stars of the day. Often, we would watch only the foreign movie, to my great chagrin. I liked Japanese Samurai flicks where a lone warrior could single-handedly slice up a horde of attackers.

Perhaps I am getting ahead of my story, but this memory of the movies is a strong one. In 1936, when "talkies" (the Japanese version of the word was "tohki") were common, Charlie Chaplin made one of his last silent films called "Modern Times". My parents stood in line at the new movie palace in downtown Tokyo to get tickets. The movie was meant to be a social commentary on the dehumanization of factory assembly lines, but all I remember is a scene in which Chaplin's crazed character went berserk and thought the hexagonal buttons on a woman's blouse were hexagon shaped nuts he daily tightened over and over. He was about to tighten her "nuts" when she ran away in terror! I was thirteen at the time and thought that scene was a riot. So much for social significance!

I now realize how splintered life was at that time, not only for my family, but for the Japanese people as well. Western culture had already invaded their ancient ways and the pervasiveness of those changes was received with mixed feelings. My sister and I adjusted to change without a care. In a way, we were Russians, but not really. In a way we were Japanese, but obviously not. We lived in a typical Japanese house with tatami rooms and yet we ate our main meals with our parents in the European manner and sat on European furniture. Unless we were with our amah. Then we behaved as Japanese children eating politely with hashi and sitting on "zabuton" (floor pillows). We lived daily in two entirely different cultures and yet it was not a burden. We were happy. At least that is how I remember those days of childhood.

My mother, always a thoughtful and practical person, decided to return to Harbin to take a series of sewing courses. It was difficult to purchase clothes for our family. We were taller than most Japanese people and Japanese sizes just did not fit us well. When my mother and sister left for Harbin, my father and I remained in Tokyo. I was six years old and ready to enter school. Nearest to our home was a Japanese public elementary school for boys.

My father took me to the school, enrolled me, and most likely was happy to find something for me to do. I was a very active child, and with my sister gone, I was probably driving him crazy.

I started school as the only "gaijin" boy in my school, the youngest and a head taller than every one else in my class. Despite my obvious "differentness", it was not an unhappy time for me. The seating was organized according to height so I was placed in the back of the classroom. The desks were designed to seat two students side by side, but because the class had an uneven number of students, I was by myself. Being shy, this arrangement suited me just fine.

In many Japanese schools, boys wore uniforms, but in ours, most wore European style clothes. Midway through the term a new boy, obviously from a traditional family, joined our class. He had a shaved head and wore a kimono. The time alone at my desk ended. This boy was always complaining and whining. One day he did something to really annoy me (I don't remember what) and I bopped him on his shaved head, causing a loud slapping sound. The little kid tried to hit me back, but he couldn't reach my head! Our teacher did not scold us. He merely asked us to stop fighting and interrupting the rest of the class. A few days later, the mother of the boy came to school to speak to me. She very politely asked me to be friendly to her son, and not to fight anymore. It made a difference. I believe I felt sorry for the poor mother (not the spoiled boy) because I never touched that boy wearing the kimono again.

A few months passed, summer vacation began, and my Pa and I left Japan to visit my mother and sister in Harbin. As I recall, my father and I stayed in a small hotel. My mother and my sister were living at my sister's godmother's house which was too small for all of us. While Lala was away with our mother she spoke only Russian. At the first meeting with my sister, I began speaking to her in Japanese, the language in which we regularly conversed. She haughtily informed me that she no longer spoke Japanese, only RUSSIAN! She was only five years old! Her haughtiness only lasted a few days and then we were back to normal.

I was fascinated by what I saw in Harbin. It was entirely different from Japan, the people, the language and the atmosphere. Although I was barely seven, I noticed the large number of Russians. Nobody was yelling "Gaijin" at me. There were street kiosks that served "beef stroganoff"—we just bought a serving and would eat it standing up. It was the most delicious "stroganoff" I ever had. To this day, it is one of my favorite meals.

Another remembrance was our swimming in the Sungari River, noted for its unpredictable underwater eddies. One day while swimming, I felt the strong underwater current pulling at my legs threatening to topple me. I held fast to the rubber float I was using, and paddled as hard as I could to the shore. It was the first time I ever felt real fear, but it was not to be the last.

My parents had quite a few friends living in Harbin and we had a lot of visiting to do. After a month in Harbin, the three of us, my father, my sister and I went back to Japan. My mother remained to complete her sewing course.

෴

THE FIRST BIG CHANGE

It was mid summer 1930 and I was seven years old. My mother had returned from Harbin after completing the sewing course. Our family was once again together and life was normal and pleasant. It was at this time, for reasons I was not privy to, my parents decided to buy a shop specializing in Russian food items imported mainly from Harbin. My father ran the shop, but continued his woolen business.

Comparing how decisions were made in my youth to today's egalitarian method whereby children are consulted about almost every aspect of family life brings a smile to my old face. At that time children were expected to be obedient, cheerful and silent unless addressed by an adult. To voice opposition to a decision made by one's father was not even contemplated, well perhaps contemplated, but quickly dismissed knowing the extreme consequences of such folly. So when my parents decided to pull up stakes and move to an entirely different neighborhood, we went and that was that.

One attraction of this move was the location of the store, which was within walking distance to the Russian

Orthodox church. My father was religious and attended services regularly. He often sang in the church choir. He had a fine basso voice and I was very proud of him. Also the shop was very close to the train station which brought many Russians to the neighborhood.

The change in our life style was dramatic. We moved from a traditional Japanese house in a totally Japanese neighborhood to a western home in a cosmopolitan area of central Tokyo. Our house had doors with hinges (not ordinarily used in Japan) and a modern bathroom. The streets were paved and there were sidewalks. We no longer removed our shoes upon entering our front door. My sister and I loved our house and where it was because we were not the only Russian family in the neighborhood, so there were many children like us to play with. We were no longer strangers.

The bustling store had a ready made clientele of talkative and gossipy Russians glad to smell the familiar aromas of their homeland cuisine and purchase the comfort food of their native land. Sundays, after church services, was always a busy time with slews of churchgoers crowding the store.

Summer passed too quickly and it was time to return to school, but not back to the Japanese one. My sister and I were enrolled in a one room school house attached to the Russian church. It was co-educational and had several grade levels in a solitary classroom. There were about fifteen students varying in ages from six to about twelve. The teacher was a small, middle aged woman with glasses, who seemed to be very smart, using difficult and long words. Of course, we were taught in the Russian language. Her husband had some minor position in the church and that is probably why his wife was hired to teach. He was short in stature, not bad looking, and evidently well educated. It was clear to all the students that this man was not someone one would wish to rile. He was very serious and stiff in his bearing always standing straight with his narrow shoulders back and his chin up. It was obvious that he had, or wished he had, a military background and considered himself in charge. No one knew what he was in charge of, but we knew he was definitely in charge of his wife, our teacher.

All the Russian families who were stripped of their homeland stuck together. They stayed in touch with each other. Little did I know as a young boy that this man would come back into our lives. The impression I had as a child of seven proved to be right. He was not a nice man.

☙ ❧

Our Own Home

A year passed. Although the shop did a good business, my parents agreed that being shopkeepers was not for them. My father's woolen fabric brokerage business was doing so well they could afford to build their own home. The shop was sold and they bought a small piece of land on a knoll near the Tamagawa River in the southern part of Tokyo. This area had been farmland, but now was being developed into residences.

Our house was not large, but designed in the Western style. The amenities were rather minimal. While there was electricity and gas, there was no water system, nor sewage system. Water was pumped from a well and toilets were Japanese style.

It was a happy time for our family. My parents' sense of pride and accomplishment most likely was transmitted to my sister and me. We children had our own reason to be happy because there were so many children to play with, all Japanese.

We had so much freedom as children. We came and went as we pleased. I don't think my mother knew where we were half the time. That is how safe it was. My sister was a great visitor. She would take off for hours and no one knew where she was. When it was getting late my mother asked me to fetch her. It wasn't difficult because I just looked for her shoes. People left their front doors open when the weather was pleasant and I could always spot my sisters shoes in the foyers of our neighbor's homes. She soon caught on and hid her shoes. That meant I had to embarrass myself by having to knock on every door and ask, "Is Lala here?", until I found her.

Among the neighbors that lived near us, I recall several vividly. One was a young childless couple, the husband being an artist who painted in the western mode. Their Japanese style house included a modern glassed-in studio with easels and painting paraphernalia. This couple was fond of us and we would often visit and watch him paint.

Down the street resided a man who sold insurance. He had a nice wife and a pretty, pigtailed daughter who was probably in her last year of high school. She liked us and would play with us in her spare time. Her father, who always wore a traditional, elegant businessman's kimono instead of a western suit, came to call on my parents one evening. I happened to be present at the time. The man started to speak slowly to my parents in Japanese hoping they could understand what he was saying. My parents were not at all fluent in his language so they always kept a Japanese-Russian dictionary handy. I sat quietly and listened as the man tried to explain the insurance policy he wanted to sell them. I understood the words he was saying, but I had no idea what "insurance" was so I remained silent. My mother hurried to get the dictionary and then quickly looked up words trying to help my father converse in an intelligent manner with this man in the dark kimono shuffling through papers all written in Japanese. The whole thing seemed very comical to me at the time. No one thought to ask me to translate. After a time and several wrong guesses and polite corrections, our neighbor finally got what he came for, my parents' signature on the dotted line of an insurance policy and I left the room.

Now, settled in our new house, my father decided that he wanted us to study music and purchased an upright piano. Both my sister and I had to take lessons. My sister took a few lessons and refused to study or practice. I, being less forthright, pretended to study. I cheated on practice time by manipulating the clock or I lied about how long I did practice. After about a year or so, my father must have noticed I was not improving and was not serious about playing the piano. And he was correct. My father repeatedly threatened and warned me that the piano would be sold. One day I returned from school and the piano was gone. I was relieved.

❦

OUR EDUCATION

When I was eight years old I began my education at St. Joseph's School, a Catholic missionary school for boys in Yokohama run by French and American Marianist brothers. This choice made by my parents literally changed my life. The next ten years created the person I became and probably should be credited with whatever success I achieved in my life. I owe my father and mother limitless gratitude for putting education before all else in my upbringing.

Because my new school was not located in Tokyo, on my first day at St. Joseph's, my father accompanied me as we boarded a local train, traveled a few stops, transferred to the main line running from Tokyo to Yokohama, then boarded a trolley to my new school. The whole trip took an hour. Seeing me settled, my father returned home. After school I went home by myself not a bit afraid of getting lost. I was elated to be independent for the first time. All my classes were taught in English, a language I did not speak nor understand. In fact, almost all my fellow first graders did not speak English, but we all spoke Japanese. At least we could communicate with each other.

Our teacher was Mr. Higly, a French Marianist brother, who seemed to enjoy children. He was an older man with a long white beard, pleasant and patient with his class of seven and eight year old boys who would not have fit in at a Japanese school because of mixed ancestry or because of being a foreigner in Japan.

Mr. Higly began teaching us English by writing simple words like CAT on the blackboard. Then he showed us a picture of a cat and we had to repeat the word several times. We learned by rote and praise. We sang songs like "Mary Had a Little Lamb" and "London Bridge Is Falling Down" that we memorized phonetically, not understanding one word of the lyrics for quite a while. I do not remember being afraid of making a mistake.

Our teachers wore black Prince Albert knee length coats and looked quite formal and dignified. When they ventured out of the school compounds for whatever reason, they wore regular black suits and always wore black hats.

Our school site was on a hillside in Yokohama called the Bluff by the foreign community. The large compound was built on a picturesque slope. The brother's living quarters and school chapel were located on the top side. A bit further down the slope was another two storied building which was built during my elementary school years. It housed a standard sized basketball court on the ground floor along with necessary lockers, showers, athletic equipment, etc. On the second floor was a fully equipped auditorium that seated four or five hundred people. It was equipped with up-to-date stage lighting, upholstered seats and a large stage on which we presented many productions. There were several stairs down from each level. The last being to a spacious flat area consisting of a two storied European style building of concrete where all our classes were held. On that same level, there was a large paved area with a big barn like structure used for assemblies and recess on rainy days. Next to the paved area was a standard sized soccer field of packed dirt, where all kinds of sports and athletic events took place. To recall my old school with its commanding buildings and grounds, that were most uncommon in Japanese schools, brings back some of the happiest times of my life. What a lucky boy I was to have been educated in such a place.

The next year my sister was enrolled in the Convent of the Sacred Heart, a Catholic girls' school located in Tokyo operated by a semi-cloistered order of nuns whose mission it was to teach girls from prominent families throughout the world. The Convent taught all classes in English with French as a second language. After one year my sister left the Convent and enrolled in St. Maur's in Yokohama so she could travel to school with me even though Sacred Heart was much closer to our home. However, I think the real reason for the change was due to the behavior of two of her classmates who were daughters of a Soviet diplomat stationed in Tokyo. My sister started using terrible language and swearing in Russian at home. When asked where she heard such profanity, she told my parents she learned it from the Soviet girls. I remember going to Sacred Heart with my father to help communicate in English. The nuns admitted the seriousness of the situation and said they would look into it. That wasn't good enough for my mother and father, who despised the Reds and decided to enroll my sister in St. Maur's located next door to St. Joseph's.

Even though my sister and I did not start school speaking English, within a year both of us became fairly adept at speaking and understanding the language. Now we spoke Japanese, Russian and English. Every language has certain words which seem to be just right in expressing what one wants to say. Often my sister and I would inject the best word in a sentence even though that word was not in the language we were speaking. One evening our family sat down at the table to eat our dinner and my father asked, "So Kostia what did you learn at school today?" My answer went something like this-(in Russian)- "We studied an American author named Mark Twain who wrote about" (in English)-"a boy named Huckleberry Finn who had"- (now in Japanese)-"many adventures and he…"

"Stop!" my father and mother said at the same time. "We can't understand you!" my father shouted, as was his way. I had no idea why he was yelling at me being unaware I was using a mixture of languages to converse. My sister began to giggle and all four of us started to laugh.

It was then that my Ma and Pa set some rules. We must stop mixing languages in our normal conversation with them because they truly could not understand what we were saying. So from that day on we spoke Russian to our parents, Japanese to our friends and neighbors and English at school. Problem solved.

The headmaster at St. Joseph's, Brother Gaschy, was an older, refined, white bearded, French Brother who had a little head twitch caused by a bomb blast when he was an officer in the French Army during World War I. In the first few grades my teachers were predominately French and taught in English. As we progressed in our grades, more young American brothers took over from the aging French teachers. The French director was eventually replaced by an American. I don't know the reason for this, but I think it was due to financial aid by the American Province, which paid for the construction of the gym and auditorium.

Another reason might have been that the older French brothers could not control the young, raucous students. Except in a few subjects like history and religion, from grade five onward we were taught by youthful, energetic, American clerics.

The younger teachers brought a new spirit to the school. Tag football was introduced, and the brothers actually played with us. Old style text books were replaced with up-to-date American ones. Our class was the largest in the whole school from the first grade through high school. The best athletes and actors were in our class. Our soccer, basketball and soft ball teams were mostly from our class, especially in the high school years. We had soccer tournaments with some Japanese universities—Japanese high school teams were no match for our teams. Once in a while we played basketball against the American School of Tokyo where we were evenly matched due to American style coaching.

Lively and energetic, we were also quite rebellious. I remember one day in our sophomore year of high school, we were reprimanded by the faculty for something we thought was unfair. That day, right after school, most of our classmates met in a little Japanese style coffee shop and decided to boycott the athletic practices, but would show up and play in the scheduled games. Naturally, we performed poorly without practicing on a regular basis. It wasn't long before there was a compromise. We all agreed, teachers and students alike, to forgive and forget. The American brothers didn't like losing games.

American movies were also shown in theaters in Yokohama. Our American teachers told us about America, but the movies showed us America and what a fabulous place it was. Since I was a small boy I had seen American cowboys and rich, happy people who lived in mansions driving big cars. Everything looked perfect in America and the good guys always won. I don't know when my family began dreaming and discussing America as a place they wanted to go. I do remember my own desire to be American and my dreams of living the life I saw in the movies and learned about from our teachers.

The year was 1931. We were secure and content. However, there were those in the world who were secretly planning treachery. It was in this year that Japan militarily invaded Manchuria for the first time. The invasion went on quietly and had little impact on our daily lives.

Yokohama was a port town located about twenty-five miles from central Tokyo, and had a significant foreign population. International steamship lines, trading and banking companies abounded, bringing many foreign families to the city. To accommodate the social activities of these diverse families, there was a large club in Yokohama, called the YCAC, Yokohama Country and Athletic Club. This welcoming and well-maintained club was used both for social events as well as several athletic endeavors, such as tennis, basketball and soccer. There were also special events presented to celebrate various national holidays. The British celebrated Empire Day; the Americans, Independence Day; the French, Bastille Day, etc. These celebrations usually involved members of the Club and their children, as well as students from Yokohama foreign schools. Depending on which country was celebrating, the programs commenced with the singing of the specific national anthems and always ended with the singing of the Japanese anthem. Foreigners behaved in a respectful manner as guests of Japan. On several occasions, I remember singing four anthems in three different languages—American/British, French and Japanese. It was all so very civilized. Everyone was getting along, or so it seemed to the average person.

In February of 1936, the young radicals in the military set off a revolt in Tokyo. There were skirmishes in the streets and the authorities shut down the city. No trains or other forms of public transportation were running in Tokyo proper. I had to get to school. My cousin took me on his bicycle to the bridge which was Tokyo's southern border. I started to cross the bridge when I was stopped by a sentry. "Where are you going?" he asked. "I'm going to school." I answered. He let me go and I continued to walk across the bridge out of Tokyo to Kawasaki. I took a train to Yokohama where I boarded a trolley to school. I arrived late and was scared to death that I would be in trouble. As I walked to my classroom, Brother Gaschy stopped me and asked, "What are you doing here? How did you get here?" "Sir," I replied "I'm late because of the uprising and none of the trains were running so it took me longer to get here. I know I am late. It wasn't my fault." Brother Gashy smiled and personally escorted me to my class. I realized later that I was the only one from Tokyo that came to school that day.

The years passed and I enjoyed everything about our school. Still being somewhat self conscious, I applied myself in my studies and did well, always trying to be at the top of my class. Scouting was introduced in my freshman high school year. I enrolled immediately. Our organization consisted of four troops, each composed of eight scouts and I became leader of one of the troops. The activities of scouting involved a lot of interaction among the members. On many weekends and some long school breaks, we would go on treks or short camping trips. All kinds of competitive games would be included in our activities.

There was one particular game that changed the way I thought about myself. This game consisted of a scout from one troop facing a scout from another, trying to make him laugh in less than one minute. Usually it was an easy effort. But there was one Filipino scout, who nobody could make laugh. One day it was my turn to take on "Mr. Serious". After several antics on my part, nothing worked. In desperation, I pulled my ears wide, stuck my tongue under my upper lip and made a monkey face. The scout master as well as the entire group burst out laughing, including "Mr. "Serious". I must have looked like a real ape! This incident proved to be very important to me. It gave me confidence—I could accomplish what others could not. This eventually led me to be the school clown and to acting in comedy performances. I eventually became an Eagle Scout.

During summer vacations, our family went to a seashore area called Chigasaki, about an hour's train ride from home, where we rented a small Japanese house. My father could still commute to work. The beach was beautiful, with fine dark sand which could get unbearably hot. Sandals were an absolute necessity on very hot days. There were several small flat reefs about a hundred yards away. On certain days when the weather was supposed to be clear, it was not unusual for people to get up before dawn to witness the spectacular sunrise. The sky was spiked with bright orange rays fanning out from a half risen sun reflecting on the calm still water. I later learned that this beautiful natural phenomenon was the inspiration for the Japanese navy flag.

I spent most of the day at the beach, coming home for a quick lunch. I would get so tanned that my teachers would comment when I returned to school.

The reefs were a very good fishing spot. It was the favorite place for older Japanese men who would sit for hours trying to catch prized black sea bream. These fish were very elusive. One would need special gear such as oiled white horse tail hair at the end of the lines and special bait of larva of silk worms. People could hire small row boats to get to these reefs. I and a few Japanese boys would often swim to these reefs and have fun, diving and snorkeling. The oldsters resented our presence because they thought we scared away the fish.

One day I decided to try my hand catching the prized fish. I borrowed the required gear and set out for the reef. I found about a half dozen oldsters already there, all in a line. I was going to cast my line close to them. They knew where the hot spots were, which varied from day to day. Before I could cast, I was chided by them and told I was not welcome. Reluctantly and somewhat miffed, I went to a spot some distance from the oldsters. Pretty soon I landed one of the prized fish. Then another! The old geezers caught none. Several of them came over with their gear. "Well", I told them—"You chased me away from your spot, do you think it fair that you now come to mine?" Grudgingly they returned to their spot grumbling about the fresh young "gaijin". I was the champion fisherman for that day. I think I caught about five.

Further away, about an hour's motor boat ride from the beach, there was a cluster of large reefs that were excellent for fishing and snorkeling. To get there, if and when the weather permitted, one had to take a boat that left only once in the early morning and returned once in the evening. The water surrounding these reefs was crystal clear. As one swam, the bottom, fifty to seventy feet below, was clearly visible and teemed with fish and all manner of marine life.

I had gone there a few times during summer vacations. If a person wanted to experience the fun of fish nibbling the line, this was a great place. You just had to cast a line and the fish would bite, although the ones that bit readily were not worth reeling in. The big desirable fish were very deep and difficult to catch.

On one of my forays to these reefs, I was snorkeling and spotted a large eel, which is considered a delicacy in Japan, some ways down. I had my diving mask and I held my four pronged harpoon with a bamboo handle so it would float in case one let go of it. I went up and took a deep breath of air, dove down, saw the eel still there. I aimed my harpoon and speared it and pinned it against the reef. Three of the prongs of my harpoon pierced the mid part of the body of the eel. To my great surprise, the eel spun around, grabbed the exposed metal prong with its fangs and bent it. It was then that I realized it was not a harmless eel, but a large deadly moray eel, whose bite is lethal. Still holding the harpoon I knew I had to keep the eel pinned against the reef for my own safety. Running out of breath, I had no choice but to let go of my harpoon and surface. Taking a short breath, I immediately looked down into the water. I could see no sign of the creature or my harpoon. I thought the moray eel had escaped with the harpoon still in it. After a few moments, I saw my bamboo-handled harpoon floating atop the water a few yards away. I swam out, grabbed it and got the hell out of there!

On these same reefs one would often see young women divers clad only in their swim panties. They were professional divers who came in a boat to pry abalone shells off the reefs, which were available only at very great depths. Women, never men, were used in this business endeavor because women's bodies could endure the cold temperature of the water. These women would dive and stay under water for over three minutes at a time, fill their bags with their catch, come up for air, take a short rest, and dive back again. After some time, they would get out of the water to rest and sun themselves—still only in their swim panties. They were totally uninhibited and all the people watching them with admiration took no notice of their bareness. I, even as a young teenager, thought nothing of it. I remember these divers as being very friendly. Once in a while they would bring up some conch or other shells and give them to me.

∞

SECOND BIG CHANGE

In my freshman year at St. Joseph's the family moved to Yokohama. Again my parents were restless and wanted to better their lives. There was a well known beauty salon for sale in the central part of Yokohama run by a Russian woman that primarily catered to the foreign community. My mother, being who she was, decided to study cosmetology in a Japanese school in Tokyo. How she learned with her limited knowledge of Japanese is beyond me. But learn she did and in quite a short time, the course was completed. She was very skillful with her hands and that probably was a big factor in getting the necessary license.

With her license in hand, my parents bought the salon in Yokohama. This necessitated our moving again. The house in Tokyo was sold and we rented a flat very close to the salon. This was a big improvement for all of us, especially for us youngsters. No more long commutes to school. We could walk to our classes in less than fifteen minutes. It took me only about five minutes to bike to school and allowed me to have lunch at home instead of taking sandwiches.

In my sophomore year something inside of me yearned to play the piano and I wanted to take lessons. I mentioned this to my father several times. His reply was usually, "You had your chance!" Not one to give up, I kept asking. One day, I broached the subject again. He asked me if I was indeed serious. I replied that I thought I was. A few weeks later, I returned home from school and in the living room was an upright piano. I started lessons at school and practiced regularly. I was not a great pianist, but I didn't care. It relaxed me and that was all that mattered to me. To this day when I play the piano, no matter how keyed up I am, it allows me to relax.

It was around this time that the husband of my teacher in the one room Russian school came back into our lives. His hatred for Communism took an extreme turn. He organized a fascist party branch that was head-quartered in Harbin and was seeking new members in Tokyo. The association attracted many former White Russian military men like my father. This Russian fanatic would come to meetings wearing a uniform of his own design featuring a swastika armband and greet the men with a stiff-armed salute saying "Hail Russia" instead of "Heil Hitler".

My father spoke often about returning to Russia after the "Reds" were defeated. I remember asking him, "When is that going to happen? When can we go?" He always answered. "Soon, I hope." Fascism was not the real attraction for most of these Russian men. It was the opportunity to plot and plan a way to overturn the Bolsheviks. My father quit the organization after a few meetings, seeing the absurdity of their unrealistic goals. His membership in this organization, even for so short a time, would come back to haunt my father years later.

❧

My Senior Year and Beyond

As early as 1937, there were clear signs of an impending war, even in my naive, adolescent world of St. Joseph's. Those signs of what was to come went ignored by most of us. Japan had already successfully taken over parts of China, first Peking in the north and Nanking in the central part. The Japanese military was puffed up with its rather easy and often brutal victories over what they believed to be an inferior people. At the beginning of my senior year in September of 1940, I was having such a good time that I was unaware of any real danger. Our American instructors were still teaching us. All twenty-six classmates were still studying, playing sports, acting in plays and having fun. Then gradually things began to change. Our class dwindled to ten students by the end of the school year. Of the remaining students who graduated, there were four Russians (all stateless), two French/Japanese, one American Nisei from Hawaii, one German/Japanese, one Chinese, and one Macao Portuguese. Slowly, one by one, the other sixteen students had left Japan for their home lands. Some left with their families. Others left with their mothers and siblings while their fathers remained to take care of business. The Nisei boy left for Hawaii right after graduation. Those of us who remained had no place to go. Looking back, I realize I was not afraid. Why should I be? I was a good student, a decent athlete, and I expected to go to college in America.

A friend of my father's, who served with him in Siberia, had immigrated to the United States soon after the revolution and settled in Seattle. They sporadically corresponded, and in my junior year my father requested a favor of his friend. Would he please obtain an application for a student visa for his son (me) in order to attend a university in the "States"? This was done and the proper application papers were filled out and sent back. We were told the visa should arrive in plenty of time for me to travel to the U.S. and enroll in a university for the 1941 fall semester. My future was planned.

On graduation day in June, 1941, wearing my navy blue blazer and white flannel trousers, I received my high school diploma. I had done well and my parents were proud of me as I was awarded special honors. The visa still had not arrived. My father's friend assured us that it would be coming any time.

In July of that year a large Japanese ocean liner, filled with passengers, left Yokohama bound for the United States only to turn around midway in the Pacific and return to Japan. Not a good omen. Was this a permanent situation? Would no more ships sail from Japan to the U.S. or was this a temporary restriction? There were many ships still sailing freely across the Pacific from other ports outside Japan like Shanghai, Manila and Singapore. My father, after some thought, decided to take me to Shanghai, where upon receipt of my visa, I could sail for the United States. Actually, the only place I could catch a boat was in Shanghai. Being stateless, I would need a visa to enter any other location. Shanghai was a free port and international city so there was no problem for me to go there.

So, in late August, my father and I boarded the "Tatsuta Maru", one of the larger liners in Yokohama headed for Shanghai. The whole trip took four days. We first sailed to Kobe, about three hundred miles south of Tokyo. We docked for a day and half, taking on many foreigners who were happy to be leaving Japan. The mood on the ship among these passengers was one of giddy relief. They did not know how lucky they were.

The only stateroom available to us accommodated four people. It had upper and lower bunks on each side of the stateroom. Our cabin mates were two American men. One man always stayed in the cabin while the other left for meals and such. The one that stayed had a large, locked canvas bag attached to his wrist. I saw them exchange this bag and lock it to the other man's wrist as they took turns leaving the stateroom. My father told me they were probably diplomatic couriers. These fellows spoke very little to us as they were obviously not on a pleasure cruise. It was pretty exciting stuff for an eighteen year old kid with an active imagination who had seen a lot of American movies.

The trip from Kobe to Shanghai took a couple of days. I was fascinated by everything on the ship—the number of passengers, the dining rooms, the decks, the sound of the sea, all of it. My favorite place was the deck where I spent a lot of time. On one of the days, as I was leaning on the deck railing, I thought I saw something in the near distance moving in the water. As I watched, a huge fish (a shark, as I found out later) came by the side of the ship where garbage was being tossed, grabbed something and bolted away. The big fish did this several times. It was quite a scene and made me think of what would happen if a person were to fall into that same water.

The sharks were not only swimming in the sea, they were on land as well. The powerful military leaders of Japan were planning what turned out be a disaster for their country and for the rest of the world.

∽✅∾

SHANGHAI, THE PARIS OF THE FAR EAST

On the fourth day we docked in the worldly, multi-cultural, multi-lingual, anything goes city of Shanghai. It was my father's first trip to Shanghai as well as mine. He had seen many places in the enormous lands of Russia as a military man, but I noted he was as excited as I when we stood on the deck waiting to disembark.

"Do you know what people call this city, Kostia?" my father asked. I shook my head. "It is called the Paris of the East. With all its sophistication and culture it is also known to be immoral and dangerous. I want you to promise me you will not associate with bad people while you are here. You have been taught what is right and wrong. Promise me." My father looked at me. We were the same height now. Eye to eye we looked at each other and I remained quiet. "Promise me." My father ordered. I answered, "I promise, Pa." Our eyes unlocked and together we scanned the impressive port of Shanghai anxious to set foot on land and experience the magic of this glittering city.

My first impression of Shanghai was its dense sea of people, all moving frantically. Everywhere, there was chaos and noise. I saw coolies in straw coned hats—everyone was shouting, rushing and pushing. The smell was a mixture of acrid cooking odors and decaying garbage. This atmosphere was a vivid contrast to the quiet order of Japan.

After what seemed an endless process of disembarking, first immigration clearance, then customs, my father and I took a taxi to the French Concession. We checked into a small, modest hotel. My father telephoned a former member of his regiment in Siberia who was expecting us, the Baron Vladimir Meller-Zakomelsky. The next day we paid a visit to the Baron and his wife, Natalia Giorgivna.

The Baron was from an old and respected family and a man who, before the revolution, was a backer of the Freeman movement that would allow the peasants to own land. He was about my father's age (mid forties), tall, thin, with a long hawkish nose and a rather protruding lower lip. His bearing was as aristocratic as his manners and speech. His wife, born Duchess Natalia Herzogin Von Leutenburg, was the daughter of Princess Olga Repnina and George Herzog Von Leutenburg. She was now known as Baroness Natalia Giorgivna Meller-Zakomelsky. Her marriage to the Baron had lowered her royal ranking. The Baroness wore no make-up. Her chestnut hair was pulled back in a severe bun. She had a plain but pretty face with classic features, soft brown eyes and a pleasant smile that she displayed often. The Baroness was fairly tall, slim, and as I recall, had a very good figure. Considering the life she and her husband were now forced to endure, she had remained quite attractive.

They lived in one room in a dog racing establishment known as the "Canidrome", where the Baron had a job as a security guard. It was located in the French Concession. Their room was about eighteen by twenty feet. It was somewhat dark, sparsely furnished, but tidy. Over to one side in the corner was a small makeshift kitchen. The bathroom facilities were down the hall and shared with several other tenants.

The Baron and Baroness graciously welcomed my father and me. It appeared that their shabby surroundings had not diminished their dignity. They were who they were and would always be—royalty. They had no children, little money, no power, no prestige and no country. Yet their demeanor was formally gracious and polite. I remember being fascinated by the contrast between their courtly manners and their humble living quarters.

Could the Baron aid us in finding a place for me to live while I waited for my visa, my father inquired. (It was obvious I could not stay with them.) The Baron replied that Colonel Apreleff, a very good friend of his from Russia, lived close by with his son, and that a room may be available there. We went to see the Colonel the next day and we were able to rent a room.

The building in which the Colonel resided was almost a half block long consisting of seven or eight sections, each with four stories and its own entrance. The street floor had a side entrance for deliveries and housed the kitchen, servant rooms and storage facilities as well as a back door leading to a small garden. The main entrance to the rooming house was on the second floor with cement stairs leading to the carved wood front door. As one entered there was a vestibule and a hallway which led to two large rooms and a bathroom. One of the rooms was rented to a Russian engineer and the other was used as a dining room. There was a wooden stairway that led to the other two floors. The Colonel and his son occupied the third floor. My father and I rented one of the rooms on the fourth floor where we shared a bathroom with another Russian fellow we hardly saw.

Colonel Apreleff was a widower and lived there with his fourteen year old son. His other child, an elder daughter, was married to one of the French consuls in the French Concession. The Colonel was about six feet tall, fit and good looking and was also of noble birth. He had been a pageboy in the Tsar's court. Later he had been a member of the elite palace guard, the Cuirassiers. I had seen pictures showing their uniforms which were extremely elegant befitting protectors of the Tsar. Their shiny, black boots were high over their knees and their tunics were white with stripes of gold braid. On their proud heads were golden helmets, topped by a long, arched plume. The person who had worn that exotic costume was now a very angry and bitter man. His exalted position had crumbled along with Tsarist Russia and he wanted it back.

As I unwind my memory tape, I realize how very plain and Spartan our rooming house was. What did I know about the life previously lived by the aristocrats with whom I was now sharing a home? I also did not yet fully appreciate how far they had fallen. It was all an enormous adventure to me.

My father, who decided to stay with me until my visa arrived, wanted me to be studying while I waited. Shanghai was home to several universities, but only three were western; St. John's University, a Methodist school; Aurora University, a French Jesuit (Catholic) institution which included a high school; and Lester Institute, a British engineering school. Arriving at the end of August, it was too late to take entrance exams at St. John's and Lester, but Aurora accepted me in every field except engineering, the very one I wanted. My French was weak and my math was not outstanding. Math was taught differently in Europe than it was by our American teachers. Europeans, at least the French, stress theoretical concepts. I did not pass the math entrance exams and I was not allowed to enter the engineering school. It was suggested that I enter the high school as a senior to improve my math and French. I thought I was not going to be there long and it would not be a waste of time for me. At least I could brush up on my French, the language spoken by all my teachers and fellow students. My visa should be arriving soon.

During this waiting time my father and I would often dine at various restaurants with the Baron. His wife never joined us. I listened to my father and the Baron sharing tales of battles won and lost while they drank straight shots of vodka. One would bring up a battlefield or comrade and the other would tell a tale. The stories were always of lost friends and dangerous deeds that soldiers never remember as heroic, but to me these former warriors were courageous men. Sometimes these dinners would last into the wee hours of the morning. One episode involving my father, stuck in my mind.

In a small town in Siberia, as the Reds and Whites were fighting house to house, my father turned a corner to find himself staring at a Red soldier pointing his gun at him. My father thought this was the end and covered his eyes with his arm. Then he heard a shot, but he felt nothing. He lowered his arm to see the Red soldier in front of him drop, shot dead by one of his White compatriots who just happened to turn the corner in time to save my father's life.

I learned a great deal about the personal hardships of the lost war and developed a new admiration for my father. It is not often that a son gets the opportunity to see another side of the man known to him only as Pa.

A few weeks passed and my father had to return home. He left me with some money for my trip to the U.S. and would make arrangements to send me a monthly stipend. My good Pa left me in Shanghai with his fellow White Russians hoping his only son would leave for America and be safe. It was the dream of all the Balabushkins to immigrate one day to America, but the confidence my father once had as a young man was ebbing. He had to face the reality of his life. He was stateless. He spoke only Russian and a smattering of Japanese. How could he make a living in the United States? He had wanted to wait until I graduated from high school, so, if worse came to worst, I could help support my family. I suppose these were his thoughts as he left for Japan in late September 1941.

❧

SHANGHAI, 1941

Shanghai's summers could get so hot that on certain days the tar on the streets melted and stuck to your shoes. The city shut down between noon and three o'clock on unbearably hot afternoons. Luckily, my father and I missed most of the hottest times because we arrived in Shanghai in late August when the temperature had cooled, if only slightly. The fourth floor room we shared was bearable, if not totally comfortable.

As I have mentioned, my father left for Japan after a few weeks. Besides the money needed for passage to the United States when my visa arrived, he left me enough money to pay my rent, my tuition, purchase school books, have my laundry done, and to pay the owner of the restaurant that delivered my evening meals. I was to receive 400 yen every month as an allowance (about $200.00 at that time, more than most men made as a monthly salary). As I recall that time of my life, the feelings of terrible loneliness come back. It was the first time I was separated completely from my family and it took some time to adjust to this aloneness. My needs were few and my allowance was more than enough. I began saving half and was able to rent a small piano for my room.

Aurora University was only a short ten minute walk from my lodgings. Every morning I would wash in the shared bathroom down the hall, dress in shirt, tie and sport coat, then leave for school. Coming from a very sheltered boyhood and educated in a Catholic boy's school by celibate Marianist brothers, I was an innocent youth when it came to girls. I was eighteen, six feet tall, skinny, and full of energy. Schoolwork always came first, and I liked sports, so girls were not really a priority as yet.

A Russian speaking Orthodox priest, who was probably British, operated a rooming house for students and young men, several of whom attended Aurora. It was a gathering place for both boys and girls to have discussions and to mingle. From what I have been told, this place was somewhat similar to college dormitories in the States. Now I had a place to go to relax and meet some kids my own age. My life was very orderly with little time to waste.

My school, my room, and the priest's rooming house were all located in Shanghai's French Concession—a territory of the French government. Shanghai as I remember was composed of five sections—The International Settlement, French Concession, Western Section and two Chinese sections, Hongkew & Pootung. The International Settlement was multi-national and I think was run by a consortium of American, British, German, and other European countries. The security for this mixture of people was shared. It all worked in concert.

The police officers in the French Concession were divided into three tiers of responsibility, the top officers being mostly French, with a few Russians and people of other nationalities. They wore blue uniforms and the stiff, "pillbox" caps made famous by Charles De Gaulle. The regular street policemen were comprised of Russian and other Europeans and wore the same blue outfit, but different head gear. Chinese officers were also occasionally mixed in to the melting pot. The third group, the ones that did the "grunt" work, was made up of Annamese (Vietnamese) who wore blue uniforms with black equatorial type pith helmets. They were all small in stature and their teeth were black, not from decay, but stained by the constant chewing of betel nuts.

In the International Settlement, the security structure was similar to the French Concession, a mixture of European officers. Their khaki uniforms were modeled on the British colonial police force. In the hot summers the officers wore short pants and high socks with garters. The guards were mostly Sikhs dressed in the khaki uniforms, but their head gear was the traditional turban. During the blazing midday heat, the Ammanese and the Sikhs were the only ones who could tolerate the high temperatures.

One felt safe in Shanghai, at least in the Western-run sections, but had to be more cautious upon entering other areas that housed many of the poorer Chinese people where one could be robbed or mugged. The social order was quite rigid, with the lower class Chinese at the bottom rung of the social ladder.

Fall emerged. Life was pleasant. I made friends, played soccer, and drank ice-cream sodas, a novelty to me. There were some dances and parties organized by Russian Clubs and church groups. The days, weeks, and months passed quickly. My life took on a comforting routine through that fall of 1941. Still no visa arrived.

December 8th (a day earlier in the States—making it Dec. 7th) is the feast of the Immaculate Conception, a holy day and a holiday at our Jesuit school. In the morning, as I was getting dressed to play soccer with my friends at the university soccer field, there was a knock at my door. I opened it to find the Colonel standing there, obviously distressed. "Japan has attacked Pearl Harbor in Hawaii. War has been declared against the United States", he said. I was silent for a moment, not knowing what to do or say. "What are you going to do?" he asked. After hesitating I replied, "I don't know, but right now I'm going to play soccer". I remember saying that. It seems so flippant and uncaring now. It surely must have seemed so to Colonel Apreleff, a man who had experienced war and had lost everything. He turned and walked slowly down the stairs. I left to play my game. I would not be going to America after all. The enormity of my situation had not yet permeated my still adolescent mentality.

The war began with a tactical and emotionally charged victory for Japan. The Japanese navy had indeed proven to be superior to the unsuspecting Americans. It was thought a fine start for the Japanese empire.

From that day on changes began to take shape, not quickly, but in a gradual, orderly manner. The Japanese forces, before the attack on Pearl Harbor, had already surrounded the city of Shanghai, and controlled it after the show of force in 1937. The International Settlement and French Concession were not bothered. Now that war had been declared, the Japanese soldiers just walked in and took over; a bloodless capitulation giving Japan one of the major port cities of Asia.

Before Dec. 8, 1941 there were about 100,000 foreigners living in Shanghai. About half of those were Russians, both White and Red (the Soviet Union was not an enemy of Japan until two weeks before Japan surrendered in 1945). Among the other fifty percent were British, French, American and many other nationals from all over the world. The Japanese authorities started sorting out "enemy nationals", citizens of countries that had declared war on Japan. These people were slowly, forcefully and systematically identified and issued red armbands with large black initials, "A" for American, "B" for British and so on. All these "enemies" were free to go about their business. Then many were accused of being spies, imprisoned and maltreated. Who knows what happened to enemy military personnel, like the few U.S. marines who were stationed in Shanghai. The Japanese were known for their cruelty to prisoners of war. The rest of the foreigners were untouched. The large French populace was not considered enemies during most of the war because France was occupied by Nazi Germany and governed by the puppet president, Petain. Stateless people like me were left alone.

Right after the attack on Pearl Harbor and war was declared, the Japanese authorities announced that all non-military enemy nationals would be interned in camps which were gradually readied. It wasn't long before all the foreigners wearing armbands disappeared from the streets and neighborhoods of Shanghai. They were not treated as prisoners of war because they were civilians and not combatants. I had been friends with a girl who was American/Portuguese and had been interned during the war. She was a slim girl when the war started. When she and her family were released after Japan's surrender, she and others that I met had become quite plump. Switzerland was a neutral nation and there were many Swiss people in Shanghai throughout the war. With constant oversight, the Swiss Red Cross had been able to send food parcels for the camp internees and made sure the food was distributed to all the prisoners. Without that oversight, who knows how these people would have been treated. There is overwhelming evidence that in other places, where enemy civilians were rounded up and put in camps, the treatment of these prisoners, especially as the war continued, was harsh, and often inhumane.

❧❧

MY LIFE AS A STUDENT GOES ON

Life in the French Concession changed little for me. The dream of going to America to study was forgotten. I received my allowance every month. I attended my classes as usual, and I continued to play soccer. The small group of Russian and French students at Aurora, were left alone, but the Chinese students, of whom there were many, had to be very careful what they said or did. Snitches and spies were everywhere to weed out "troublemakers". The Imperial Japanese Army did not really have much to worry about. A large part of China was under Japanese rule and China's only hope, General Chiang Kai Shek, was far, far away in Chung King. He was certainly no threat to the Japanese occupiers in Shanghai.

The city was actually booming. There were no shortages of any kind. All one needed was money and I had enough, thanks to my parents' generosity. I began asking girls out for dates. Nothing serious, but I was beginning to realize there might be something I was missing. It was at this time that I first began to be concerned about my family. I had not heard from them for a time, but soon letters arrived and my worries subsided.

The young man that shared the fourth floor with me, left. It seems his father, who was supporting him, was a merchant seaman stranded in Singapore and could no longer send money to his son. His room was not empty for long.

The Baron and Baronessa Meller-Zakomelsky, my father's old friends, arrived with their belongings. For them the room on the fourth floor of the rooming house was a big upgrade.

The Colonel had in his employ a Chinese cook who prepared the morning and evening meals for him and his son, Peter. Because the Baroness had to prepare meals for her husband, she politely suggested to the Colonel that she would be happy to also cook for him and Peter, for an appropriate financial arrangement, of course. I too, was invited to partake of the Baroness's culinary efforts for a fee. Dinner was now provided. As might have been expected, the Baroness was not an outstanding chef, but she was able to produce healthful, plain meals for those at her table. The local restaurant no longer catered my evening meal and I no longer dined alone in my room. My dining experience was significantly altered from then on. More about that later.

∽✢∽

THE VICTORIOUS JAPANESE—1942

Fist, I must describe the mood of Shanghai in the summer of 1942. The Japanese Military was piling up victories and advancing everywhere they struck. The few pro-Japanese groups in Shanghai were ebullient mostly because they collaborated with the occupiers for financial gain. Even though Japan was an ally of Germany, there were diverse points of view tolerated openly regarding the war between Germany and the Soviet Union. Both countries had agents to spread propaganda in China, especially in Shanghai. Remember, Japan was not at war with the Soviet Union at that time. The propaganda tactics used by both sides were varied and sometimes sinister. One example comes to mind. There were several movie theaters in Shanghai, some pro-Germany and others pro-Soviet Union. One could go to one movie theatre to see a foreign film. The accompanying newsreel would portray a battle where the Soviets appeared to be winning. At another movie theatre across the street, the same battle would be shown in a pro-German newsreel describing the courageous fighting of the German forces! The Japanese, Germans, and the Soviets all had their own propaganda machines, trying to put the best spin on the flexible facts. A dramatic example of divergent reporting was the massive Battle of Stalingrad, which lasted months. The Germans showed their initial successful advancement on the city, occupying ninety percent with Russian soldiers dying by the tens of thousands. When the tide changed, the Soviet's newsreels were finally able to show the enormously successful conclusion of that historic battle and the surrender of hundreds of thousands of German prisoners. The Germans could not make that loss a victory no matter how hard they tried so they did not show the battle at all in their newsreels. The Japanese propaganda was easy to advance to the Chinese populace since their written language was the same.

✑

ENTERING ST. JOHN'S UNIVERSITY AND A VISIT HOME

The school term ended in early summer of 1942. I had graduated from Aurora High School, received my Diplome D'Etude Secondaires (Equivalent au Baccalaureat Francais), but again I did not make my math grade. I decided to change schools. I took the entrance exam for St. John's University located in the Western Section of the city. I passed and was allowed to enroll for the fall semester in chemical engineering.

Obtaining a visa to go to Japan was not difficult at that time so I was able to return home for a two months vacation with my family. They were doing well thanks to my father's practical preparation before the war started. Anticipating shortages of goods was bound to occur, my father stocked up on woolens he purchased in Nagoya, where most of the textile factories were located. My sister, who had graduated from St. Maur's convent, was informed that her school would be closed. In fact, all foreign schools were shut down, including my old school, St. Joseph's. With hardly a whisper the value of money began to erode, but it had not yet made any appreciable difference to us, and my family didn't seem to notice the difference. I was having a good time in Japan seeing old friends, swimming, going camping; the same fun-filled activities that I was used to doing while on vacation.

But I could sense a change was in the works. In spite of the all the news of success being touted by the Japanese press and government, we all knew that everything was not going so smoothly. I noticed all types of stores and food emporiums were sparsely stocked. Goods, including food, were rationed. The people on the streets were no longer dressed in the newest styles and the happy, confident faces I had seen before were now devoid of smiles. The city had taken on a quiet and somber mood.

The foreigners who were not interned were constantly being watched. One had to be careful of what one said or did. Every foreign family was visited on a regular basis by Japanese security agents trying to extract information, opinions and whatever else they could learn. An incident that happened on a camping trip with two friends that summer is a good example of Japanese spy fever.

We had gone by train to the Japanese Southern Alps and had to get permission from local authorities for a five day jaunt, which we obtained easily. On our return trip, we were met by several "Kempetai" (Japanese Secret Police) at the end of our train ride in Tokyo. We were asked to step inside a room in the station. There were three men--one officer, one ordinary soldier and a man who was most likely a civilian police detective. The young soldier took our knapsacks and thoroughly examined the contents. The officer in charge sat down at a desk in the middle of the room and started to interrogate us.

"Please give me your travel documents." He began without looking at us. The detective sat next to the officer and also asked us questions. This went on for almost two hours. During that time the young soldier sat silently with his sword placed between his legs and his hands placed formally on the hilt of the weapon.

"Could you please tell us why we are being questioned?" I said in Japanese. We just went on a camping trip. We did nothing wrong."

The officer looked at me, "You speak Japanese very well. Why is that?"

I explained that I was raised here and was on summer vacation from University in Shanghai. That did not seem enough for the policeman.

"Your permit is for five days. Why are you returning after only four days?" he asked in a tone Japanese men use to impress other men with their authority.

I decided to be very respectful in my demeanor so we would be released.

"Sir", I began, "We ran out of food so we had to return. That is all there is to it."

The officer told us to wait and he and the detective left us with the young fellow holding the sword. The minute they left the room the young soldier leaned back, relaxed his arms and put the sword against the wall. "You sound like you had a good time, but you ate too much."

He said laughing. We spoke a bit until we heard the other two approaching. The young soldier rearranged himself, we stood and the officer handed us our papers with a grunt. They kept the roll of undeveloped film that was in my friend's camera. Eventually the developed film was sent back to us.

The summer of 1942 ended and I returned to Shanghai to begin my engineering studies at St. John's University.

⁂

LIVING WITH NOBILITY

Have you ever had the sense that everything you believed in, everything you expected to last and never change was gone and there was not a damn thing you could do about it? Those most likely were the thoughts of these nobly born people who were now left without a shred of their former grandness. They all agreed that their country and their way of life was destroyed by a group of Godless creatures who brought chaos and destruction to a cultured civilization respected all over the world. To murder the Tsar and Tzarina was one thing, but to slaughter their innocent children was unforgivable.

These feelings of loss showed themselves in different ways with skewed levels of fury and acceptance.

If I close my eyes, I can still see the dining room as it was so very long ago. The dining table was made of dark wood to seat eight, but with only six chairs. The seating was as follows: The Colonel sat at the far end of the table; the Baroness's place was at the other end of the table closest to the entrance to the dining room; I sat on the Baroness's left and young Peter sat next to me on his father's right; the Baron sat opposite to Peter and me.

Only now do I wonder if the seating was according to protocol or rank.

Dinner was announced at approximately 6:30 in the evening and we would all sit down. The table was covered with a white linen cloth with napkins at each place. On the table was salt, pepper, bread and butter. Soon the Baroness, wearing a long cotton apron, would arrive with a tray of food in serving bowls that she had carried up from the first floor kitchen. No one seemed to take notice of this. If needed, she would make other trips until all the dishes were on the table. None of the men seated offered to help carry the platters of food. They all seemed to ignore this poor woman going up and down the stairs carrying their dinner. Perhaps the Baroness was spared the indignity of serving if no one took note of it. In my home I would have offered to help my mother, but here I behaved as the other men did. When the platters of food were all placed on the table, the Baroness would leave, and return, her apron removed. The Baroness was no longer the cook or server. She was ready to be seated. We all stood while the Baron held his wife's chair. She sat down and a short prayer was recited. Then the Colonel said, "Baronessa, may we start?" With a nod of her head and a gracious movement of her small hand, she replied, "Please begin". This ritual never varied.

The conversation was about the news of the day. War and politics were common topics. Peter was asked about his day at school.

The Colonel was rabid to the point of pure loathing in his feelings for the Bolsheviks. He rooted for the Germans not for any other reason than vengeance. His hatred was without restraint for those who were traitors to the Tsar and Mother Russia. His only son, Peter, was a student at a German school most likely overseen by the Nazis where he wore a uniform of military khaki and a red armband emblazoned with a black swastika. On days when Peter did not have time to change his clothes after school he arrived at the dinner table wearing that costume.

It is part of this narrative that I tell the truth about those times. I have met many people from Germany who say they had no idea what was being done to the Jewish people and others branded as parasites by the Nazi regime. I was not in Germany, but I was in Japan and Shanghai and everyone knew of the atrocities happening in the concentration camps everywhere in Europe. It was in the newspapers. Shanghai had a considerable number of Jews who had arrived as early as 1905 and another large contingent who came in the 1920s. Those who were long established in the city were referred to as "Shanghai Jews" identifying them as established citizens well known in business and the arts. Many had come from Russia to escape the pogroms and then the Bolsheviks. The final group was able to escape before being taken to the camps. I was happy to accept the warm hospitality of at least one Jewish family whose daughter was in one of my classes at St. John's University.

In 1943 I sat with this boy who acted, as far as I could tell, proud to wear his Nazi uniform. No one at the table objected, including me. I remember thinking the boy was a fool, but he was only fourteen and greatly influenced by his father. Most Russian military men had no love for the Jewish people. My own father had said to me more than once, "They refuse to fight for Russia. What kind of man won't fight for his country?" Anti-Semitism was rampant. Without it Hitler could never have become the exalted and beloved leader of Germany. I was not immune to the prejudices so embedded in those at that dinner table, but my views were slowly being expanded as I met and became friends of those who were so despised in so many parts of the world.

So we all sat at the table and conversed like the well-educated, cultured people we thought we were. The Baron and Baroness were happy the Soviets were not winning, but they never gave any indication they were Nazi sympathizers. I noted that these dispossessed nobles hoped and devoutly prayed for the return to the glory of Imperial Russia when the Soviets were defeated.

Invariably, at the end of the meal, the Colonel would ask "Baronessa, may I smoke". He would light up and start smoking, which he seemed to enjoy very much. This behavior was repeated every evening. Conversation would continue for a while before the group disbanded. The Baroness cleared the table after each meal and most likely washed the dishes in private in the kitchen below.

As I listened to those conversations nightly, I came to realize why the Russian Revolution was inevitable. A huge proportion of the land was owned by people like those with whom I was dining. The peasants were nothing more than indentured slaves who were kept ignorant and powerless. Although the Tsar had started redistributing land, it proved to be too late.

I did not hate the nobility, but I was very sympathetic to the cause of the under-classes and despised the gross injustice they suffered. Like most young people, I was very altruistic even though I also hated the Reds.

Perhaps, because of these thoughts, I never called the Baroness by her preferred title. I addressed her in an acceptable, polite manner, which was Natalia Giorgivna, but I never addressed her by her title "Baronessa". Russian tradition dictated that middle names of both male and female children were based on the patronymic system—meaning taking one's father's first name. For example, my father's first name was Polycarp—therefore, my full name was Konstantin Polycarpovich Balabushkin and my sister's full name was Ludmila Polycarpovna Balabushkina (note the male and female endings). Neither the Baroness, nor anyone else at the table, insisted that I call the Baroness by her royal title, but I felt the Baroness was a bit slighted by my perceived lack of proper distinction.

While the Baroness was pleasantly chatty, the Baron was quiet, one might even say, meek. He opted out of most conversation preferring to listen. The Colonel, on the other hand, was outspoken and behaved in a manner mirroring his former elevated status. His fury was at times evident and he rarely smiled.

The Baron, Baroness, the Colonel and Peter spoke fluent French and peppered their conversations with French idioms and quotes. I was able to keep up with the conversations, because my French was now up-to-par due to my attendance at Aurora University. Even though my family was not from royalty, the Baron respected my father as an officer, so I was accepted into this regal company just as they graciously accepted my payment for room and board. Circumstances had changed and all the White Russians had to change with the times or perish. The strong ones coped in whatever way they could.

Despite my less than reverent attitude, the Baroness seemed to like me. Often she would stop me when I returned from my classes and tell me stories of her childhood and young adult years.

"I lived in a beautiful palace with eighty rooms that were filled with lovely French antiques. The walls were covered in silk from China. In every room there were exquisite paintings done by old masters. We had so many servants, one for every room. Oh, and the parties and grand balls my parents would host for hundreds of guests. My ball gowns were made in Paris." Her voice seesawed between elation and sorrow as she treated me to the stories of her former life. Other times she would tell me how she and her whole family would spend their summer holidays at luxurious resorts on the Black Sea. "We played tennis and croquet and rode horses. Every one was there for the season. Royals from all over Europe." Only once did I see her eyes brim with tears as she spoke. Rather than let me see her cry she turned away for a moment, controlled her emotions and turned back to me smiling. She said she was a first cousin to the Empress Josephine, Napoleon's wife. "I have the dress Josephine wore at her wedding to Napoleon and letters written to her during the Egyptian campaign." The Baroness told me. I was more than a bit skeptical, although I said nothing. The Baroness, perhaps perceiving my doubts, set a day and time for me to see her treasures. When the time came for our meeting, I knocked on the door to her room and she told me to enter. Standing there in that plain room was the now beautiful former duchess wearing Empress Josephine's wedding dress. The dress was a very pale blue satin with a train and long tight sleeves. I was awestruck! The transformation was remarkable. This slender woman, who just a few minutes before was just another modestly clad woman no one would have noticed passing on the street, was now a beautiful lady. I could not help myself from staring. I imagine my response was very reward-ing to the baroness. After a short chat she showed me two large, solid gold candelabra and two tall, crystal vases that were said to be wedding presents to Napoleon and Josephine. As she sent me on my way, she handed me two letters written by Napoleon to Josephine during his Egyptian campaign.

I sat on my bed afraid to unfold the stiff yellowed stationary that I held in my hands, the same paper held by one of the greatest generals of all time, Napoleon himself. I was aware that my hands were touching a part of history. I slowly opened the letters.

The letters were written in bold black ink with wide, slanted penmanship. They told of battles in Egypt, success and a longing to return home. Affectionate expressions were written in a formal way, but with the comfortable sharing of intimacy that I supposed was common between a man and wife. I was quite moved as I carefully refolded the letters and returned them to the Baroness who was again in her somber dress, in the world in which she was forced to live. I realized that despite humiliating hardship, some things are kept until there is nothing else. Those personal treasures were proof of what once was. The hope of restoration to that life of privilege was still alive in the patient, yet pitiful hearts of these Russian nobles. It was a special compliment to be trusted with the tangible proof of the privileged past of the Baroness who desperately wanted her life back. In my heart I believed she would be gravely disappointed.

ఎఇ

CURFEWS AND LONELY SOLDIERS

Shortly after December 8th, 1941, the city of Shanghai was cordoned off with barbed-wire fences that were open during the day allowing passage in and out of the city and closed again at night. A curfew was enforced for everyone. The fences closed off all roads in and out of the city at nine P.M. Travel through these barricades after nine P.M. required special passes. One evening I took a walk to visit some friends who lived not too far away and stayed later than I should have. Returning home, I found barbed-wire rolled across the street. On the other side of the barricade were two young Japanese soldiers who, as I approached, pointed their rifles with fixed bayonets at me. Their duty was guarding the entrances to Shanghai. They hollered at me in Japanese that I could not enter after curfew. Acting innocent I politely spoke to the guards in Japanese and said I was sorry to be late and was not aware of the curfew. As usual, Japanese coming from a westerner was a surprise and immediately sparked questions. I explained my background and what I was doing in Shanghai. As luck would have it, one of the soldiers was from Yokohama. He asked me where I had lived, even what street I lived on. He immediately let me through the fence, but would not let me go home insisting I stay for a while and talk with them. I suppose they were both lonely and wanted to talk to someone about home. After some time, perhaps an hour, they let me go with a friendly smile, picking up their guns and being soldiers once again.

Another incident happened when I had to pick up a parcel that my parents had sent me from Japan. I had to go to the main Post Office that was located in Hongkew, a Chinese section of Shanghai across a creek that divided the International Settlement and Hongkew. There were three bridges connecting the sections. Only one could be used by foreigners, and naturally the Post Office was farthest from the foreigners' bridge. The trolley I took to get to the post office ended right across this bridge. Grudgingly I used the authorized bridge which took me at least twenty minutes to reach the post office. After picking up the parcel, because it was bulky and heavy, I decided to try crossing the nearest bridge which was much closer to the trolley I needed to take to get back home. A sole Japanese Marine guard dressed in his formal blue uniform was standing mid-point on the side of the bridge. As I approached he pointed his bayoneted rifle at me motioning me to go back. Again pretending ignorance, I asked in Japanese why I could not pass. He was mildly surprised, put his gun to his side and relaxed. Then he began to ask why I spoke Japanese.

After explaining, as in the former instance, he made it clear that he wished to talk to me for a while. In the meantime, the Chinese, who were waiting to cross the bridge, took advantage of the guard's distraction and crossed it as quickly as possible. Even in times of war, most human beings need comfort and normal conversation to survive the ordeal.

It was time to return home to Yokohama for the 1943 summer vacation break. Travel documents were now difficult to acquire. When I went to the Japanese authorities to get my visa for Japan, the man in charge, who the year before was dressed nattily in western clothes with his hair long and smooth, was now in an olive drab suit that had become standard civilian attire. His hair was cropped very short like a soldier's. He recognized me from my previous visit when he was polite and friendly. This time, his attitude was quite different. He started lecturing and reminding me that there was a war going on and travel was restricted. In spite of this, he issued me the necessary papers warning me that I might not be able to get back to Shanghai. My guess is that the reason I was able to travel at all is because all Japanese highly respected students.

The journey was more complicated now because of the danger of American submarines believed to be in the waters we were traveling. We arrived in Nagasaki without incident and I had to go through the usual formalities—immigration, customs, etc.

"Why are you entering Japan?" one officer asked.

"I am here to visit my parents in Yokohama." I replied. Not once did my ability to speak Japanese as a native go unnoticed by a Japanese person. It always made it easier for me. It seemed they were more able to trust me. In my baggage was a black case containing my trumpet that I played in the orchestra of the university. Of course the inspectors asked me to open the case. Seeing the trumpet one of them said, "Do you play this instrument?" I told him I did.

"Play something for us." he said with a hint of a smile.

"You want me to play here in the Customs shed?" I asked.

"Why not? Play for us."

And so I blasted a few numbers for them. They seemed to enjoy the concert and let me go.

From Nagasaki, I took the train to Moji, a northern port of Kyushu Island, where I had to transfer and purchase an express ticket to Yokohama. Leaving my baggage on the elevated train platform, I went down to the train station to get an express ticket that I could not get in Nagasaki. Before I reached the ticket office, I spotted a police booth. Knowing I would be interrogated by the policeman inside, I went in. He could not see me as he was holding a newspaper in front of his face. When I said "Moshi Moshi"(Hello), he put down his paper and stared intently at my western face. Speechless for a moment, he asked, "What are you doing here?" I told him politely in Japanese that I needed to get an express ticket. He looked at his watch, said there was plenty of time, sat me down across from his desk and after examining my papers and seeing they were in order, began a conversation. Tacked up on the wall at the side of his desk was a large map of the Far East. Pointing to the area conquered by the Imperial Japanese military, he asked, "What do you think of our conquests?" In my youthful recklessness, I said nonchalantly "Great, if you can keep it!" I will never forget his long silence. I feared that I had definitely made a big mistake in saying what I had said and in such a disrespectful tone. To cover up my error in judgment I innocently smiled at the officer. It seemed to work. I was lucky. The policeman let me go after personally getting the express ticket for me.

On the train trip to Yokohama, the last leg of my trek, I couldn't help but notice a mild looking, smallish man wearing a plain, baggy suit and a felt hat. He was walking up and down the aisles of the train and would sneak a glance at me every time he passed. Later he stopped by my seat as though he was going to speak to me. Before he could say anything, I smiled and asked him in Japanese, "Are you a member of the secret police?" He was somewhat ruffled that I was so blunt, but he took out his credentials and showed them to me. I had guessed right. In fact, he probably thought I could be a spy, and it was his duty to check up on me. He sat down across from me, removed his fedora, and asked me a few necessary questions. I suppose my answers reassured him because he then relaxed and we began a nice conversation which kept both of us entertained for quite a while.

During the train ride, at several intervals, all the passengers were ordered by the conductors to pull down the shades on one or both sides of the train. It was obvious we were passing industrial war plants or factories. We continued chatting until the little man put on his hat, wished me well and disembarked midway to Yokohama.

Finally I arrived home to find the conditions dire. Now all goods were rationed. Beauty salons, massage parlors, entertainment places and other businesses considered unnecessary to the war effort were closed. People on the streets wore serviceable drab clothes, their faces steely. The mood in Yokohama, as in all of Japan, had become stoic. Still, the Balabushkin family was together again and thankful for that blessing.

My father remained enterprising. He had come to own four or five chickens that laid eggs daily and on occasion he would trade the eggs with the local pharmacist for pure alcohol. He then created potent vodka that he sipped on a daily basis like the true Russian he was.

Our family loved animals and always had a dog for a pet. When our pooch died of old age, my sister begged for a new dog and the family obtained a young German shepherd she named Rex. It wasn't long before the feeding of the dog became a problem. While on a visit to the vet, my sister mentioned the problem of feeding the dog. The vet informed her that German Shepherds were eligible to get their own rations from the local authorities. Lala applied and obtained the canine rations. No one told us that by accepting rations, our pet could be drafted. Shortly thereafter, a written summons arrived requesting that the dog be brought before a canine review board. There were about seventy dogs of various breeds at the meeting out of which nine were taken into the Japanese Military Canine corps. Rex was one of the nine. German Shepherds were used as carriers of medicine to the battlefield medics and as messengers to the front lines. We heard later that Rex was a casualty of the war. We all loved that dog, but my sister loved him the most. I was only with him for one summer vacation, although I was the one who trained Rex. I can see why he was drafted. He was very smart and learned quickly. I wonder if my sister would have applied for the rations if she knew the consequences.

With summer over, it was time for me to return to Shanghai and to my second year at St. John's University. One of the members of the Secret Police who was assigned to watch our family was a frail, old man like most of the agents not fit for military duty. On one of his visits he warned us that if I returned to Shanghai, I may not be able to get back to Japan. My education was of prime importance to my parents, so it was decided that I would return to Shanghai. Before I left, my father gave me a small bar of platinum to take with me. The Yen now had very little value in China. If I became desperate, I could sell the platinum for my livelihood. I put the small treasure in a vest pocket in my suitcase for safe keeping.

My generous father also gave me his beautiful gold Swiss watch on a solid gold chain that was his most prized possession. This goodbye was in the fall of 1943 and I was not to see my family again for many years.

With my belongings, I took the train to Nagasaki with a transfer in Moji, to board the boat to Shanghai. I lined up to go through the customs. The officer asked me to open my bag. I remembered that I had put the platinum bar in my vest pocket. Knowing that gold and platinum were considered contraband, I realized how stupid I was.

First a sweater was removed, then a few shirts, a couple of jackets. Next was the vest. The custom officer stopped and began to put the clothing back into the suitcase and closed it. Trying not to change my expression and outwardly calm demeanor, I breathed for the first time in what seemed like an hour, and boarded the ship.

It may seem to you that I had an inordinate amount of luck. I suppose it is true at that stage of my life. Being a student and not yet a full fledged adult was taken into account by those who questioned me. I was a brash young man seasoned by years of not showing fear or kowtowing to anyone, although, I was always careful not to be rude or disrespectful. Self-confidence was a trait admired in Japan by both men and women. So perhaps luck was not the only thing that saved me from disaster. It was one factor, but luck is fleeting and as the war continued luck was not enough to keep me alive.

The journey back to Shanghai was long and arduous. The boat zigzagged to avoid American subs and the China Sea was rough. Smoking at night on deck was strictly forbidden. I was the only foreigner on the ship. My berth was in front part of the boat and I felt every movement of the ship causing me to be very sea sick. The air on the deck of the ship made me feel better, but as I walked the deck everyone watched me. "Who is this gaijin? What is he doing here?" their eyes seemed to say. No one spoke to me and I did not attempt to speak to them. It was only a two day trip. "Who cares what these people think?" I thought to myself. I was greatly relieved when we docked at our destination. That same ship was torpedoed by an American sub on a voyage sailing back to Japan from Shanghai. I returned to St. John's.

In my old age, looking back on my early life, I have become aware that I am relating these stories as an aloof observer rather than a person who is emotionally attached to the country and people of Japan. I did not realize this while I was living through those tragic times. The truth is my family and I were always set apart. We did not belong. No one was rude or unkind to us and we were courteous and friendly to all the Japanese people we knew, but we never considered Japan our "home". Japan is where we lived. Russia was "home" to my parents. I had no home.

❧

EVERYTHING GETS WORSE

From the fall of 1943 when I returned to Shanghai, to the early spring of 1944, life in the city remained constant. Those of us with enough money lived fairly well and became used to the inconveniences caused by the war. The poorest Chinese already had nothing and many began to slowly die. Starvation, disease, and exposure all took its toll, and before long, bodies appeared on the sidewalks of Shanghai. It was horrible to see people lying in the streets with open wounds, mothers holding their emaciated babies in their arms, wailing and begging. I would be in the International Settlement for one reason or another and would see a ragged, skinny person lying dead or dying on the pavement. As the mild weather of spring ebbed and the temperatures dropped, more bodies appeared. Hand-held carts were used by city employees to collect the dead as well as the nearly dying.

I remember one day, my friend, Walter and I were out walking. One of the body collectors was picking up an emaciated body whose eyes rolled and whose arm moved. Walter, who spoke some Chinese, said, "What are you doing? That man is still alive!" The worker shrugged and replied, "He'll be dead soon, so what's the difference." We dared not confront these body collectors. One critical word could spark a riot. We both turned away full of fear and sickened by the sight. The lightness of innocence was being replaced with the darkness of reality. My heart and mind were numbing to horror and I was getting use to seeing suffering on a daily basis.

As 1944 rolled into spring, four hundred Yen bought half of what it did in 1942. Food became my first concern. I could no longer afford the dinners provided by the Baroness and my rent also became a burden, necessitating my sharing my room with Walter. To supplement my meager funds I began tutoring foreign, mostly Russian, high school girls, primarily in math, ironic as it may seem. It wasn't long before the allowance that my father sent me was worth almost nothing and lasted less than a week. I wrote my father and told him to keep his money that was still worth something in Japan. This period of my young life proved to be a test of endurance, of hunger, and the witnessing of the true consequences of war. The skinny, shy, studious, and even religious boy I was when I landed in Shanghai faded and finally disappeared as my belly became empty.

I started to notice that the well-to-do and even the clergy I would pass on the streets had full, fat stomachs. While on those same streets, bodies of the dead and dying were pushed to the sides waiting to be carted away. I had seen these sights before, but only when my own stomach ached for food did I feel and fully understand the pain of others. It was then that reality became personal. It was at this time that I stopped being religious, having lost respect for the hypocritical clergy who had taught me to "love thy neighbor" and "have pity on the poor". My prayers went unanswered so I stopped praying.

Despite being hungry most of the time, I kept going, at least during the day when I was busy. Late at night when I laid in my bed in the dark, I could not always push the fears away; fears that I would never see my parents and sister again, that I would never finish school or even that I would die. Those terrible thoughts invaded my mind and like physical pain became magnified in the night.

One day as I walked across a crowded street following a tutoring session, holding the handlebars of my bicycle, I felt the cold air against my back. My coat kept out the wind, but my stomach let out an angry growl from lack of food. The school books I carried back and forth from my classes at St. John's University were stuffed in a leather bag in the basket of my bike. It was close to Christmas in 1944. I was so tired, living day to day wondering how long I could continue to go to classes, pay rent and have enough money left over for food.

I looked around for the little Chinese kid who was always running up to me with his hand outstretched, "Shi san, Shi san (mister, mister), he would call. He was a cute little boy not more than six or seven. I gave him a coin when I could. During the warm weather he would run, but as the weather turned colder his gait slowed and his young voice weakened. I hadn't seen him for a while and I worried about him because he was getting thinner and thinner.

Every day I saw the same sights over and over. Bodies covered in rags leaning against the side of buildings, some dead and others almost dead. Where was that little boy? Every day was the same, but on that particular day for some reason, perhaps because I was so tired, the stark horror overwhelmed me. As I rode my bike an image came into my mind. In it, I was standing in our family living room in front of my father who was furious. I was sixteen and had done something to really rile him, most likely talking back, and knew I was going to be slapped so I put my hand to my face to ward off the blow. "Take down your hand!" my father shouted. I let my hand drop while I stuck out my chin defiantly. The slap came, but it didn't hurt as much as I thought it would. It turned out to be the last time my father ever hit me.

Strength comes from odd places in one's consciousness. I began pumping the pedals of my bike faster. I clenched my jaw, stuck out my chin into the cold wind with renewed defiance. I decided to survive no matter what.

While poor Chinese people were dying, the rich did well. Others did well also. A plump Chinese man in his typical blue Mandarin collared, ankle length tunic with long wide sleeves would lead a string of hand carts, pushed by coolies, that were loaded with frozen pigs or other merchandise. This train of hand carts was quite a sight and occurred on a daily basis. At several points along the streets, there would be policemen on duty checking permits of the owners of the merchandise. As the Chinese man approached the policeman, usually at a street corner, he would raise one of his arms leaving his long sleeves dangling. The policeman would pass by and put his hand in and out the sleeve in such a manner that was hardly noticeable. The string of carts would pass by without a pause. The policeman would stand around nonchalantly for a while, then would take off his cap, put his hand into it as though he needed to air it and put it back on his head with the bribe inside. Down several blocks, this scene would be repeated with the next policeman. This went on until the goods reached their destination. It is a wonder that after a day of accepting all those bribes that the caps fit on the policemen's heads.

Sometimes, the police would stop people for no apparent or justifiable reason. The quickest way to resolve any matter, whether legal or not, was to offer a bribe. The tactics used by the policeman would first be of consternation. How dare anyone think he was dishonest and accept a bribe! He would then suggest going to the police station, which, he politely said, would take too much time. The policeman would then take the person to the side, and "kindly allow" that person to leave after reluctantly accepting a "gift".

Thievery and crime were rampant. Beggars, pimps and pickpockets were everywhere. I was victim to pickpockets twice, in spite of constant warnings. The locals were much more wary and were less victimized. On one occasion my stolen wallet was returned by someone who had found it on a street—minus the little money I had.

One sunny summer day, I was with a local Greek friend walking on Bubbling Well Road in the International Settlement. It was a busy shopping area, dense with pedestrians. My friend suddenly turned around, chased a Chinese man, grabbed him by his collar and yelled something at him. The Chinese man meekly surrendered the fountain pen that he had picked from my friend's shirt pocket. I was amazed at this fast reaction and asked him how he knew he was robbed. His explanation—the way he was bumped.

One learns from experience. Some time later, I accompanied a friend to the Canidrome, not to gamble, but on some business that he had there. While exiting through the crowd, I felt a peculiar sensation at my jacket pocket. I automatically smacked my hand on the pocket and felt a hand pull away. Most pickpockets were scrappers who would filch your wallet and run away. No one ran. A well dressed Chinese man was standing close to me acting like nothing had happened and pretending to look at the race results. I thought he was the one I had stopped, but so what, he didn't get my wallet. I was learning.

Mainland Japan was being bombed by the Americans. It began slowly and escalated in frequency. No letters were getting through, to nor from Japan. I had heard that the women and children were moved out of the larger cities to safer places in the country. One of the last letters I received from my parents let me know that my mother and sister had found a little house in the mountain resort area of Lake Nojiri, located about 150 miles north of Tokyo. All the able-bodied men, including my father, were ordered to remain in the cities to act as home guards, manning sand bags and water containers. But as 1944 ebbed, I heard nothing from my family. As those days and nights replay in my mind I feel like I am holding my breath. Short words. Short phrases and sentences; that is all I can manage to describe what it was like and explain, even to myself, how I coped with the idea that my family was possibly gone. Emotions that one is expected to experience when life turns dark can be avoided, stored in ice, maybe never to be melted. I think that happened to me. My heart and soul became cold as solid blocks of ice. It took decades for them to thaw.

Classes continued. The piano was long gone. My trumpet was sold. The piece of platinum was sold. My father's prized gold watch was hocked several times and finally sold. I was lucky if some of the parents of the girls I tutored asked me for dinner or tea after the tutorial was over.

Walter, my roommate, and I had a little Hibachi grill in our room where we would concoct soups for dinner made with whatever ingredients we could afford. For breakfast we ate black bread spread with lard and sprinkled with salt. When we had any money, which was almost never, we would buy a bowl of noodles from a street vender and together with the Chinese, eat it standing on the pavement. My skin started to turn yellow from lack of proper vitamins. I brushed my teeth with salt. Clean clothes became less of a priority because the very cheap laundry service became a luxury. The tuition at St. John's University was paid first from whatever money I could earn from odd jobs. I was still able to purchase used books or borrow them from a fellow student.

In spite of the dire circumstances, life went on. Walter and I would sometimes be invited to dine at the home of a friend's family. We would, as inconspicuously as possible, gorge ourselves at dinner. There were occasional lectures, dances and other gatherings where snacks were served. Sometimes those snacks were the only food we ate that day. It never occurred to us to ask for help or let anyone know of our plight. It was our problem, not anyone else's.

At St. John's, we made many friends, both European (non-enemies of Japan) and Chinese. There were about seventy European students. Most did not mingle with the Chinese. I had played trumpet in the university band and was an ardent badminton player, the only westerner who took part in these two activities. Most of the badminton group consisted of "overseas" Chinese, from places like Singapore, Indonesia, Borneo or Thailand. They were a different breed from the local Chinese. I easily made friends with the "overseas" Chinese because they considered me like them, an overseas student. On many an occasion Walter and I would be invited to their entertainment events, where we would take advantage of snacks that were served.

❧❧

SVEN, THE POLICEMAN

My friend and roommate, Walter, was good looking as you can see in the photos. He was a bit taller than I with dark wavy hair and skinny like me. He did not give a damn about personal neatness and would sometimes not bother to take his underwear to the very cheap Chinese laundry. He would rummage through his dirty clothes and find something that was the least soiled. He was an intelligent but easy going guy. I was intense. The old saying, "opposites attract" was true in our case. Walter had lost interest in his studies and was not attending classes at St. John's on a regular basis. We were both weary of our low-down situation and we were ready to do almost anything to improve our lives and to fill our empty stomachs. Before we were forced to sell everything we owned just to exist, both Walter and I had commuted to the university on our bicycles. Walter had a German bike made by a company called "Adler" which was the "Mercedes" of bicycles and the envy of all. I had a Japanese made bike I had brought from home.

One day while we were leisurely pushing our bikes in the French Concession, we encountered a policeman at the corner. He was a lieutenant, a Russian, and his name was Sven. He was of medium height, a little shorter than both of us, but solidly built. He admired the Adler and began a conversation. When he found out that I was from Japan, he told me he had a brother living there who was working for the Japanese government. It seems his brother was a genius with languages and could read and write Chinese, Japanese, Russian, French, German and English and had been a professor in Harbin. The Japanese "offered" Sven's brother a job in Tokyo. I am sure he had to accept the offer.

When I left for Japan for my 1943 vacation break, Sven asked me to take a small parcel to his brother. I never met his brother, but my father knew of him, so when I arrived home, my father delivered the parcel for me. When I returned to Shanghai I brought a letter to Sven from his brother.

Sven began trusting us after that. As things started to get worse, we heard a rumor that there was a possibility of secretly going to Chungking. General Chiang Kai Shek was resisting and fighting the Japanese with the help of the U.S. forces. We were told that if fellows like us made it to Chungking, the U.S. military was more than willing to welcome us into their group of fighters. We had heard that some Russians from Shanghai had gone there. It was a dangerous trip because the Japanese patrols were everywhere. We mentioned to Sven our desire to go to Chungking to join the U.S. Forces. He then told us that he was an underground operative working against the

Japanese in Shanghai. Some time later, when we bumped into him again, in early 1945, he said there was an opportunity to go to Chungking. The deal was that we had to drive a truck load of hand guns collected by the underground in Shanghai to Chungking. We would be paid the enormous sum of US$20,000.00 for this, collectible at the destination or in Shanghai. All along the way we would be directed by the Chinese underground. They would guide us, hide us, and help in every possible way. Dangerous! Yes! Possible! Yes! I imagined Walter and me evading Japanese patrols as the Chinese underground led the way onto unknown side roads with our truck filled with guns.

"20,000 dollars! My God, that is a fortune!" I said to Walter. "What do you think? We can leave Shanghai and really do something important. And we can get rich at the same time."

Walter looked at Swen with that familiar grin on his face that I had seen so many times when I was overly excited about something.

"We don't know how to drive." That's all he said.

Eventually, Sven told us that there was one Russian dare-devil who took the job, made it back to Shanghai, collected the fortune and lived it up for a long time.

Who knows how my life would have turned out if one of us knew how to drive a truck.

∽℘℘

STEALING TO SURVIVE

Winter settled in and fuel was scarce like everything else in 1944. Bamboo fences were everywhere surrounding various buildings and houses in the French Concession and other sections of Shanghai. The fences started to disappear. People were stealing them for fuel. Walter and I became very adept at rolling up those bamboo poles without getting caught.

Coal was prevalent, but so expensive that the Chinese people began to granulate the coal and make patties. The patties burned fast, but they were cheap and allowed one to cook a meal.

When we began stealing and did not get caught, we were emboldened to take bigger risks. It wasn't long before an opportunity arose, allowing Walter and I to come into some much needed funds. A former lower-classman from my old school, St. Joseph's in Yokohama, had moved to Shanghai before the war, and worked as a night watchman for a Japanese navy garage. He had noticed that Chinese workers were pilfering gasoline by pouring it in square, five gallon tin cans with handles and sneaking it out at night. When my watchman friend told us about this, we thought we could cash in. I still had my bicycle and Walter "borrowed" the Baron's bike, (the "Adler" was long gone). The bicycles had racks over the rear wheels. The operation went as follows: we would ride our bikes to the garage very late at night and wait in the shadows. Our friend would whistle as a signal that all was clear. He would bring out two cans and we would strap them on our bike racks and race home! We had to take safe routes home not to get caught. But in one of our raids, the gas can fell off my bike rack, making a huge noise and spilling some of the gas. I heard people's voices and took off, raced to a hiding place and watched as the Chinese police picked up the gas can. They looked around for the culprits they most likely thought were Chinese, and I was able to escape.

Walter and I did not overdo these forays although it was a temptation. The money we acquired from selling that gas, split three ways, (my old schoolmate got his cut.) kept us going. We soothed our consciences by rationalizing that we were aiding the Allies and the war effort! Obviously, we were never discovered.

Good luck is a powerful ally. We took so many chances. It was exciting to live on the edge. I can understand how criminals get addicted to danger and the feelings of exhilaration that comes from beating the odds. And yet, despite our success, I decided stealing was not a good career choice.

THE JAPANESE AND THE JEWISH PEOPLE

In the late 1930's, thousands of European Jews were fleeing Hitler's atrocities and pogroms. Many escaped as best they could and when they could. The fortunate ones were able to leave early on. Millions never made it and we know what happened to them—concentration camps, forced labor, gas chambers.

I was told that sometime before the bombing of Pearl Harbor, two ships, each carrying about six hundred Jewish refugees had sailed from Europe, either via the Suez Canal or around the Cape of Good Hope, bound for the Americas. The Atlantic Ocean was too dangerous to cross because of German U-boats. Before they reached the Pacific Ocean, they were intercepted by the Japanese navy in the waters around occupied Singapore. These ships were ordered to sail to Shanghai where all the passengers were taken to Hongkew. One can only imagine the thoughts of those people as their chance for escape was seemingly thwarted. When the passengers disembarked they were surprised that they were left alone to fend for themselves. They were allowed, with some restrictions, to go about their business and live their lives as best they could, but I believe, they had a curfew and had to be back in Hong-kew by midnight. It is interesting to note that the Jewish people I spoke of who had come earlier and were respected citizens of Shanghai were not restricted at all.

For most of the war the Japanese government refused to cooperate with Nazi Germany's constant requests and threats concerning the Jewish residents of Shanghai. There have been many books written about this act of defiance by the Japanese and the reasons put forth may vary. However, the fact remains that the Jews in Hong-kew were not murdered by the Japanese.

Another sad incident occurred one day when U.S. bombers, aiming at a Japanese air base just outside Hong-kew, miscalculated and the bombs hit the predominantly Jewish section killing about two thousand people, mostly Jewish refugees who thought they had found a safe haven in Shanghai.

∞∞

PLANES ABOVE US

Shanghai proper was not a target for the Allies to bomb because there was really nothing there, no war related factories, and very few Japanese forces. The Allies also were thinking ahead to the time when the Japanese would be defeated and were not about to destroy the port of Shanghai. Also the Allies were very aware of the many westerners trapped there. By the end of 1944 and early 1945 when it became apparent that the Allies were winning the war, occasionally to taunt the Japanese, a lone, small, American fighter plane, flying too high for the anti-aircraft guns to reach, would appear from the clouds and skywrite a big "V" in the sky. Once or twice, a plane would skywrite "U.S.A.". We could hear the Japanese anti-aircraft guns, and see smoke puffs in the sky. I am sure those brazen acts by American pilots drove the Japanese crazy.

A little later the American planes began bombing the areas surrounding Shanghai where the Japanese military did have air bases, material warehouses, and other installations. Most of these raids were at night. We would climb up on the tiled roof top of our building and watch the fireworks—tracer bullets trying to reach the bombers and bright explosions as the bombs reached their targets. We always knew when an actual air raid was about to occur. Our rooming house was close to the edge of the French Concession and was near to an airfield. First we would hear the Japanese planes' engines revving up to take off in order to escape the possible bomb attack, then we would we hear the sirens and then the air raid would commence. The roar of the incoming American bombers was followed by the staccato of the anti-aircraft guns and finally the sounds of destruction as the bombs exploded.

In Hongkew, bordering the Soochow Creek next to the Garden Bridge, there was a twenty-two story skyscraper called the Broadway Mansions, overlooking the "Bund", which was the water frontage road of the International Settlement. A few days after the skywriting, Walter and I were visiting friends in Hongkew. We were returning home when an air raid siren blared. It was a nice cool day with some low clouds. We ran into the Broadway Mansions building to get off the street only to find the elevators not working. Just before the air raid siren, the Bund was bustling with businessmen, vendors, bicycles, rickshaws, coolies loading goods on sampans. In no time, after the siren, the area was empty. We found the service stairs and bounded up to the twentieth floor where the steps ended. Looking out the windows we witnessed seven American fighter planes in perfect formation swoop down from the clouds on several Japanese navy vessels docked on the Whampoo River. They appeared one at a time. After each plane dropped its bombs, it turned sharply, zooming upwards, the belly of the planes passing right in front of our viewing place. Meanwhile, the Japanese soldiers, two floors above us were shooting anti-aircraft guns at the American planes. Every time an anti-aircraft gun went off, the displacement of air caused us to be sucked away from the open window where we were watching. The results of this mission were mixed for both sides; not one American plane was shot down and not one Japanese ship was sunk. Those who took the brunt of the raid were unlucky enough to be in junks on the Whampoo River. The raid ended and we carefully made our way down the stairs. We survived while many of those innocent people trapped on junks died.

My wife has asked me how I felt while I witnessed such destruction. Was I afraid of dying? The truth is I do not remember how I felt. It was exciting. I remember that. Perhaps terror is tamped down by rushes of adrenalin. I don't know. I just don't know.

༺༻

THE WAR IS OVER

In the beginning of 1945 everyone in Shanghai was aware the war would soon end. Germany was being invaded by the Allies and it was just a matter of time before Hitler and the Nazis would be forced to surrender. The Japanese forces were losing all that they had gained and were in retreat. The long, treacherous, bloody battles in Guadalcanal, the Philippines, Okinawa, and Iwo Jima took enormous toll in men and armaments. The Samurai philosophy that had so permeated the military leaders would not permit surrender. Every soldier must die fighting or commit suicide rather than lose face and shame the Emperor by laying down his arms in defeat.

When the first atomic bomb was dropped on Hiroshima in August 1945, everyone was shocked by the massive destruction caused by the new weapon. Most of the population in Shanghai despised the Japanese invaders, but the enormity, magnitude, power and the utter devastation one bomb could cause stunned everyone. The Japanese hierarchy mistakenly believed the U.S. did not have another bomb. When the Japanese would not agree to the unconditional surrender demanded by the Allies, a second atomic bomb was dropped on Nagasaki. Now no one doubted the all-encompassing supremacy of the United States.

The use of the Atomic Bomb was probably the most important and controversial event of the 20th century and changed the world forever. It took a short time for the actual surrender to be signed, and finally the terrible fighting and carnage was over.

The use of the atomic bomb was a decision that will be debated for years and years and one that placed President Harry Truman not only into the history of the United States, but into the history of the entire world.

If you lived in Japan at that time and saw the suffering caused not only by the bomb, but by the arrogance and pride of a few men, maybe you would determine that the dropping of the atomic bomb was a direct result of that pride. Who should shoulder the blame for killing so many human beings? I personally am grateful to President Truman for making that fateful decision. History has shown that the Japanese would never have surrendered unconditionally and it took a second bomb to finally convince the Emperor to end the war. If the war had continued, I believe the whole country of Japan would have been destroyed and my family would have perished along with so many others.

By the end of the war, the Chinese money was deflating by the week. Paper notes were in ten thousand denominations. A loaf of bread cost Yuan 6000.00, a cup of coffee around Y 1000.00, etc. The price of everything was going up. Businessmen had to hire coolies as well as armed guards to haul money in large containers to the bank.

My graduation from St. Johns University was without pomp. I received no congratulations or handshakes. I didn't even pick up my diploma. I was alone. I did know what had happened to my family. Again I pushed those fears away and buried them in the dark, deep hole of my soul along with all the other inhuman acts I had witnessed.

❧❧

i)   My father – 1920
ii) My mother in school uniform
iii) My father and mother –young married couple
iv) My father with former aide Kamkin

i)   Family portrait 1927
ii)   Typical "Japanese children"

i) Formal family portrait 1931

i) My first school experience 1929

i) First grade at St. Joseph's with Brother Higly
ii) Being coached in American football at St. Joseph's

i) Boy Scout bugler 1940
ii) Acting in high school production
iii) Biking to school – Yokohama 1939 – Vorobiov, me and Walker

i) St. Joseph's athletic field
ii) and auditorium

i) High school graduation class 1941
ii) My graduation photo

i) First house built in Tokyo 1931
ii) Second house build in Tokyo 1949

i) Mother attending beauty school in Tokyo 1938
ii) Mother's beauty parlor

i) Lala at St. Maur's High School in Yokohama 1940
ii) Lala post war Japan
iii) Rex, the family pet, conscripted by Japanese military 1943

i) Student at St. John's University – Shanghai 1942
ii) Walter with his "Adler" bike and me 1942

i) St. John's University – Shanghai 1943

i) St. John's University badminton awards 1943

i) U.S. Auxiliary Military Police (AMP) – Peking 1946 – 1947
ii) At Austrian barracks in Peking
iii) AMP outing in Peking
iv) Inspection at AMP ammunition dump in Peking

i) Me at 145 pounds in 1954
ii) At 180 pounds during treatment early 1955
iii) At 220 pounds finally well 1955

i) Eric Crane – Tokyo 1948
ii) Konwal Co. office with "Boon"

i) Konwal Co. office with Mr. Shimizu
ii) Relaxing after hunting 1949
iii) Dancing at U.S. Army club

i) Ginbasha Night Club 1956 with friends
ii) Ginbasha Night Club with Chiyo and Yoshi 1956

i) Farewell crowd at Tokyo airport before departure to U.S.
ii) PAN AM plane to U.S. 29 January 1957

i) My wife, Arlene, 2009

SOVIET SOLICTATION

While the war raged, most Russians in Shanghai were White refugees with a few Reds. We really did not know who was what. However, after the war it became apparent who were the Reds.

The Soviets were trying hard to convince White Russians to consider returning to Mother Russia where life would be wonderful and all Russians would be welcomed with open arms. Being university educated and speaking four languages, I was a prime target. A lot of pressure was put on me to become a Soviet citizen. So much so that I wrote my father telling him that many White Russians in Shanghai were considering the tempting offer. I must admit I fantasized about what life would be like as a big shot in the Soviet Union. In a letter to my father I asked for his opinion. My father's response was short and sweet, "Wait until we can talk in person". Knowing my Pa, that was 100% notification to me not to fall for the Soviet line. There were many young people who did fall for the Party line and made the decision to leave China and go to Soviet Russia.

Before and during the war, Shanghai had many European clubs to meet the needs of the western populace. They were run by the different ethnic groups. The French club was the largest and most prestigious, occupying nearly a whole block. When the war started, the British and American clubs were closed. The Russian club, composed almost entirely of émigrés, was in a fairly large, though unimpressive, building, in the French Concession. All kinds of events took place there. The president of this club, a long time resident of Shanghai, had held his post for quite a number of years. He was very active in helping needy Russian refugees and was greatly respected by all the members. He had two children who were students, a boy and a younger girl, whom I knew and socialized with regularly. Right after the war ended it was revealed that this well respected man had been a Soviet undercover agent. Even his children were not aware of this fact. It was very hard on the children of that man. No one held it against them, but they were most uncomfortable in our company following this disclosure. Most likely, the family returned to Russia.

Boris, my friend from St. Joseph's, had gone to a university in Manchuria. He also was proselytized by Soviet agents. They did their job very well and convinced my friend to go "home" to Mother Russia. His story is worth telling.

❧❧❧

BORIS

Those attending St. Joseph's grammar and high school in Yokohama were mostly boys of mixed parentage, but in our class there were four stateless Russian boys: Serge Petroff, the son of a general; Dimitri Vorobiov, the son of an aviator; Boris Ogorodnikov, the son of an officer; and me, the son of a cavalry officer. All our fathers fought in the revolution against the Bolsheviks. We stuck together, as one would expect, because of our common heritage. The best athlete and the best looking was Dimitri. Serge liked to act in the dramatic performances our Marianist teachers produced. He was also an athlete and cheerleader at our games. Boris and I played sports and often had roles in our school's many plays. We were all good students.

Boris, like me, was one of the thousands of Russians born in Harbin. He was a chunky fellow with wavy brown hair, a broad Slavic face, red cheeks, bright blue eyes and a ready smile. It was easy to see why this only child was cherished by his parents. Boris was a popular boy with a taste for fun. And we all had plenty of that!

I recall an incident that may describe how much fun we had. It was during a dress rehearsal of the school's comedic production of "Julius Caesar". I was playing Caesar and Boris was Marc Anthony. In the scene where Anthony stands over the dead body of Caesar, Boris was supposed to wipe his tears with a towel or handkerchief. In one of our rehearsals, he had soaked the cloth with water to simulate tears. This little addition was not part of the script. I was so surprised when the cold water hit my face that I got up and kicked Boris in the behind, then quickly laid back down as if nothing had happened. The art director and some of the teachers that were there roared at the bit and it was incorporated into the run of the play.

Those happy days of youth passed and we soon were young men on graduation day at St. Joseph's High School. In 1941, Serge, Dimitri and Boris remained in Japan while I went to Shanghai to await my visa to enter the United States to study.

Boris applied to a Japanese university in Tokyo, but although he spoke Japanese fluently, he could not read or write Japanese well enough to be accepted. His parents, wanting him to be safe and sensing war was possible, encouraged Boris to enroll in a Russian university in Harbin, Manchuria, where his classes would be taught in Russian. That decision would prove to be the first snow flake that began a huge avalanche of unfortunate events.

The Soviets declared war on Japan two weeks before Japan surrendered and occupied Manchuria. With the end of the war, Boris ended up living in the Soviet controlled zone. It was at this time that his parents petitioned the Soviet Embassy in Tokyo to allow their son to return to Japan. Their petition was denied.

Serge and Dimitri ended up in Allied controlled Japan. I ended up in China which was an ally of the U.S.

If we, as young men in Japan and China, were pressured to become Soviet citizens, you can imagine what it was like for Boris living alone in Manchuria under Soviet domination now knowing he would not be allowed back to Japan. He was courted and praised and manipulated by the Soviet propaganda agents. I can understand why he succumbed to their pressure and promises. He was comfortable in Harbin surrounded by his own kind. Why not take the job offered to him by the Soviets. We are all Russians after all.

Boris was called into temporary service by the K.G.B. (Soviet Secret Service) in Harbin for a short period. Soon thereafter he was transferred to Siberia where he became a radio commentator broadcasting Soviet propaganda in English to Far Eastern countries. All copy that he read on the air was written for him by the Soviet propaganda machine. During this time he was doing pretty well financially. The Iron Curtain had dropped with a loud thud. Boris could not get out of the Soviet Union, so the elder Ogorodnikovs gave up a comfortable life in Japan to be with their only beloved son in Siberia.

Boris eventually met and married a pretty physician named Nina and they had three children. He always said that meeting his Nina in Khabarovsk and having his children were the only good things that happened to him in the Soviet Union. Some time later, he was transferred to Moscow, where he continued as a commentator, beaming the same propaganda to English speaking countries in Africa.

If you knew Boris as a young boy you would understand how terrible it was for him living in the Soviet Union. He was a happy go lucky fellow and not at all political. He was religious. The few freedoms that had been allowed after the revolution were erased after the Second World War. Everyone lived in fear. The grand ideas of the Marxists proved to be a sham and the Soviet ideal was reduced to rhetoric and distrust of everyone. Boris did what he was told and played by the rules.

Many years later when Boris and I met again he told me with tears in his eyes, "The thing I regret most was that my parent's lives were mired in hardship because of me."

I tell this story to illustrate once more how good fortune has played an enormous role in my life. I doubt I could have accepted my fate as well as my friend did. Thank God and my wise Pa I never had to find out.

❧

THE ALLIES ARRIVE IN SHANGHAI

Within weeks after the official surrender document was signed between the Allies and Japan, a few American military personnel appeared in Shanghai. The first Americans I saw were four or five airmen riding down the main thoroughfare of the French Concession in an open Jeep. When I and other pedestrians on the street saw them, we cheered and yelled, welcoming these heroes. They were taken aback with all the attention, but got into the celebration by waving and enjoying the moment.

One of the first changes initiated by the American and Chinese authorities was replacing right hand drive used in England, to left hand drive used in the States. They did this with amazingly little inconvenience, traffic snags or accidents. One day the trolleys and busses were running one way and the next day they were running in the opposite direction. How easy it is to insert major changes in the way citizens live when there is no discussion.

There were serious concerns among the Allies and the Chinese military that riots and looting would occur. Japanese soldiers were ordered by the Allies to remain in Shanghai before the arrival of Allied forces to keep order and prevent any disturbances. These soldiers, in their Japanese uniforms, stood on all the main streets of the city in a line about thirty to fifty feet apart with weapons ready. They took a lot of verbal abuse from local passers by, but they held their post in unflinching silence. Within a brief period, upon the arrival of more allied forces, the Japanese soldiers were finally released from duty and sent back to Japan.

One day, I arrived home to find a phone message from some American Major. I didn't follow up on the call thinking it was a mistake. I did not know any American military people. A couple of days later I happened to be home alone when the telephone in the hallway, used by everyone in the building, rang. I answered the phone and heard a very upset person on the line. It was that same Major and he really let me have it for not returning his call. He was calling from the Red Cross with news of my family and strongly suggested I come to see him immediately. I rushed down to Red Cross headquarters and learned that my parents and sister were alive and well. There was no postal service between China and Japan at this time. The Major was kind enough to send my letter to my family through the U.S. military postal service. We had not communicated in over two years. Feelings of relief and homesickness swelled up in me, but it was not possible for me to go home to Japan. The authorities were allowing only military personnel and necessary civilians to enter occupied Japan. Soon after, U.S. Forces arrived in Shanghai en masse. Walter and I made friends with many service men. They were kind enough to mail my letters to Japan through their postal services. My sister did the same in sending letters to me.

It didn't take too long after the surrender for Shanghai to come back to life. The mines placed in the Whampoo River were removed and the American navy was able to sail into Shanghai bringing troops and needed supplies. Shops, businesses, bars, restaurants started to open for business once more. It wasn't long before all hell broke loose. American sailors walked down the gangplanks of their ships into the city of Shanghai and took over. All their pent up energy emerged in a giant wave of exuberance resulting in complete pandemonium! I can tell you any chance of getting a date with a Caucasian girl was greatly diminished if not impossible.

Gangs of street urchins would swarm around them, begging for alms or cleverly picking their pockets. Rickshaws had a heyday charging exorbitant fares taking the sailors on circuitous routes around the city. Walter and I languished on the sidelines while the hordes of Americans made Shanghai their personal playground.

I watched the American forces arrive in their crisp uniforms riding in Jeeps and trucks. Then I saw the Chinese troops arrive in air transports. One day I happened to be at the main airport and saw Chinese troops disembarking. As they stepped out of the planes they were sprayed with disinfectant to kill the fleas and lice on their tattered uniforms. They carried their belongings and supplies on bamboo poles like coolies. These were the brave soldiers who fought under General Chiang Kai Shek. The contrast of the two victorious armies was a precursor to the future.

Mao Tse Tung, the charismatic and powerful communist leader, and Chiang Kai Shek, the nationalist wartime leader, were already starting the struggle for the ultimate control of China.

The U.S. and its allies were desperately trying to get the two Chinese political entities to form a coalition government. They set up an operation in Peking to do this. It was called the Peking High Command, with a large number of high ranking U.S. officers. This group of officers was sarcastically referred to as: "The Temple of 400 Sleeping Colonels". There was very little to do for the U.S. officers, and the nickname given to them was referring to the famous statues housed in the "Temple of the 400 Sleeping Gods", a park museum some distance outside of Peking. Ironically one of the "gods" venerated in the temple was Marco Polo, although one could not tell one statue from another. Mr. Polo looked just like the other "gods".

In 1946, a guy like me didn't know, nor much care, who was going to take control of the vast land of China. White Russians despised Communism and most of us had no respect for Chiang Kai Shek. I, like everyone else who had survived the war, was weary of turmoil and fighting. Getting a job was my top priority in the fall of 1946. There were no jobs for chemical engineers, mechanical, yes, but the Shanghai that was the Paris of the Far East had disappeared. The American Army was hiring and I was one of the first in line for a job—any job.

AUXILIARY MILITARY POLICE

The American GI's who were serving as the regular Military Police guarding military installations and supply depots were completely overwhelmed by the thievery of the poor Chinese. Anything that was not nailed down was taken, and even if it was nailed down, the thieves found a way of stealing it. One cannot blame those who stole because it had become a way of life during the war as I well knew. Peace did not change anything. The Americans in command decided to form a civilian Auxiliary Military Police force consisting mainly of former Shanghai policemen, but also of other men who wanted or needed a job, like yours truly. Walter and I applied and were hired. We were issued American army uniforms with a special patch marked AMP in large blue letters placed on the upper left sleeve. One could not distinguish an AMP from a regular U.S. GI, except for the AMP patch. We were assigned to guard the living quarters of the U.S. military, supply depots, PXs, ports and all the other places where pilfering was taking place. As I recall there were about two hundred AMPs working for the Americans of which about half were Russians. As mentioned earlier, the value of Chinese money was steadily eroding. My monthly salary as an AMP was Yuan 3,500,000.00, which was about US$ 125.00. I was a millionaire!

I was assigned guard duty at a military garage. I still did not know how to drive. However, during the night shift, I was taught how to drive a Jeep, then a PC (personnel carrier) and finally I learned how to drive a truck.

I thought a driving job would be better than guard duty so I asked for a transfer, took the necessary test and began driving guards to and from their assigned posts. I liked the job, but there was a lot of lag time between posting and collection shifts.

After driving the four o'clock to midnight shift to their respective destinations I was returning to our post. It was late and the streets were deserted. Driving a little faster than usual on the narrow street, a small bundle appeared in my headlights. Trying to slow down I realized the bundle was dead baby that had been thrown out on the road. I managed to steer so the bundle was between the wheels of the truck. There was no space to go around it. I did not stop.

I know this is a terrible story. In the world in which I had lived for too many years, the sight of a dead baby thrown into the street was a sight one would see several times a month. No one picked up these often bloody bundles. Sometimes these small corpses were the results of self inflicted abortions. I tell this story to describe the culture in which I had unwittingly become a part. Unwanted babies, mostly females, were routinely discarded like garbage and indeed were picked up by the garbage detail of the city, throwaway human beings not worthy of care or even life.

The officer in charge of our unit was a young American lieutenant from Shaker Heights, a posh section of Cleveland, Ohio. He was bored because there was very little work for him to do. One day, while we were chatting, he asked me if I played chess. I was not a good player, but I knew the game. The next day he brought a chess set and during the down times of our day we would play chess in his office to the annoyance and envy of the other guards. He was quite a good player, and being competitive, I improved. We ended up being friends and he invited me many times to join him at the Officers' Club or a café for coffee. It seemed to me that soldiers with no war were like firemen with no fires to put out.

Our AMP headquarters for operations and assembly was at the port closest to the Bund. One day after finishing driving the shift change, I walked out of our building, to get some fresh air. There were bales stacked in rows, cases and cartons of U.S. military supplies being sorted and loaded onto trucks by Chinese workers. I saw one of our AMP guards. Being curious I asked him (he was a veteran of the former French Concession Police Force), how the coolies got away with so much theft while there appeared to be so much security. Just about then a whistle blew, signaling the ten or fifteen minute morning break for the busy coolies. They gathered in a row and lounged against piles of bagged supplies and started smoking and sunning themselves. The guard told me to watch them. Many of them were holding their cigarettes in one hand, while the other hand was behind them. After a few minutes, the coolies would start heading for the rest rooms one by one. The guard followed one of the coolies, searched him and found a U.S. military shirt hidden under his sweater. One of the coolies had evidently cut one of the bales, took a shirt and passed it along behind the line of the smoking men. The thieves passed the stolen goods through the men's room window facing the street where their pals waited.

Shortly after, the lieutenant from Ohio was transferred, and for a while there was no replacement. In the meantime, the head office of the AMPs needed someone with experience in typing. I had received an advanced certificate in typing while I was at St. Joseph's, and I got the job—which was titled "Operations Sergeant". This job lasted a few months, until it was decided by the brass to transfer many AMPs in Shanghai to Peking.

❧

A New Job In Peking

The Allies had pretty much everything under control in Shanghai, but Peking was a different story. The U.S. Army needed some trained civilian policemen in Peking for security detail, as thievery was rampant and out of control there. The Peking Command decided they needed about one hundred forty people for the project. They requested seventy of the Shanghai AMPs and the rest of the force would be hired locally in Peking. The Shanghai group included twenty-five Indian and Pakistani AMPs to specifically guard a large ammunition dump about thirty miles outside Peking.

I was asked to join the Peking project and I accepted. My job was to continue to be a sergeant in charge of Operations. A former Russian policeman, a Red, was hired as a lieutenant. He had been a sergeant with the French Concession police for a very long time and was experienced in his field. We knew each other, but we were not buddies. I did not like him, but it didn't matter because we did not work together. This fellow was a tough guy in his mid-thirties with a thick, stocky build. His hair was red and he sported a "Clark Gable" style mustache that was auburn in color. The mustache did not improve his looks.

The seventy selected AMPs from Shanghai were to be transported to Peking by U.S. military planes in two flights. The equipment used was a B-46, a cargo plane that carried about fifty or sixty people. This was to be my first time in a plane and quite a thrill. I was to go with the second group which was delayed a few days due to weather. When we finally arrived in Peking, I found that I was not in charge of Operations, the job for which I had been hired, but instead assigned to guard duty at supply depots.

The Red Russian former policeman had put his communist buddy in my place. That did not sit well with me at all. This guy was now my boss. We were supposed to be a team, each with our own particular responsibilities. I went to him and asked, "What is going on? I was hired as the Operations sergeant and you gave the job to someone else!"

"What do you mean, 'what's going on?' You were late getting here and I filled the job. That's what going on!" the Red lieutenant answered me.

"You had no right to do that. You don't have that kind of authority." I said raising my voice.

He shrugged and dismissed me with a wave of his thick hand.

My first thoughts were, "Who does this jerk think he is?", but I knew better than to say this aloud. This guy outweighed me by at least thirty pounds and if he hit me I would hit the ground and never get up. So I left and went directly to the American officer in charge at the Peking Military Headquarters and told him I wanted to quit. I explained I wasn't hired as a guard. "My contract says I was to be an Operations sergeant and that's the job I want." I said as calmly as possible. "What do you think?" the officer said. "We didn't fly you here for pleasure!"

There was another officer in the room who was listening to the whole encounter and turned to me saying, "Wait a while before you quit. We will look into this." Up to this point, in the formative stage, we did not have a full time U.S. officer assigned to us. I left the office and returned to guard duty.

I got a taste of what guard duty was like. The hardship posts were gasoline depots, freight stations, supply depots, etc. The desirable ones were U.S. buildings, both military and civilian, PXs, and such. The hardship posts were especially tough in winter because the guards were out in the open with no shelters, while the desirable posts had guards inside heated buildings.

Soon thereafter, an American captain, named Hussey, was assigned to oversee our operation. There were several meetings during the week, with the captain meeting with various people in our group. We did not know what was going on. A little while later, roll call was held. We all stood there while Captain Hussey announced that a few changes were being made. I was to be the new sergeant in charge of Operations. My friend, Walter, was designated as one of the sergeants. A new lieutenant was nominated—an older resident of Peking. He had been a colonel in the White Russian army and was hired more as a ceremonial figurehead than leader. He could hardly speak English.

"What about me?" asked the Red lieutenant. Captain Hussey looked at him for a moment and in a commanding manner he calmly replied, "You're fired for taking matters into your own hands and disobeying orders."

The Cold War was starting even at a common roll call in Peking. The Red lieutenant was flown back to Shanghai a few days later.

That story did not end that day. It was up to me to assign the daily posts and duties for the one hundred and forty men in Peking. I tried very hard to be fair and not show any favoritism. The episode with the fired Soviet was not forgotten. I heard rumors, that some disgruntled Red AMPs believed I had engineered the whole plan. It got back to me that there was talk of getting rid of me permanently. I dismissed the talk as drunken palavering. Later I found out it was not all talk.

It was one incident that probably changed some of the Soviet policemen's ideas about me. Barrels of gasoline were starting to disappear from a small fuel depot that was guarded by our AMPs. The depot was quite a distance out of town in a barren, deserted location—a very undesirable and strenuous task for our guards, especially in freezing winter. The barrels were stashed in long rows and difficult to track at any one time. The criminal investigators for the U.S. military asked me who I thought was doing the stealing. I was asked if it was possible that our guards were responsible for the thefts. I told the officers, yes, it was possible, but there was no proof. What I didn't say was there were plenty of rumors going around that a couple of the guards, whose names I knew, were involved in the thefts. Was I supposed to act on rumors? I did not give their names to the officers. I chose to let the investigators investigate. I suppose word got back to those that wanted to kill me that I had kept my mouth shut and did not divulge their names as primary suspects.

᪣

PEKING, THE ANCIENT CITY

Now that my job was secure, I was able to explore the magnificent city of Peking. The ancient art treasures were everywhere as well as the architectural marvels created centuries before.

The walled city of Peking (meaning North Capital) was large and shaped like a rectangle. The shorter sides of the rectangle faced north and south, with the longer sides east and west. The whole city was surrounded by stone walls that were very high and very thick. There were four massive wooden doors, one each on the four sides, to access the city and were guarded day and night by Chinese soldiers. Entrance and egress after midnight were limited to official business. Centuries ago the walls had been built to protect the city from bandits and incursions. The population inside the walled area now numbered in the hundreds of thousands. There were several very wide and long streets running north and south, east and west. The widest of these streets was in front of the famous Forbidden City where the Emperor and his many concubines had lived. It was now a compound with palaces, shrines and museums where a young man like me could imagine the exotic, luxurious and isolated rulers of old world China. The side streets called "Hutungs" led to enclosed housing compounds. It took me many visits to experience the vastness of the mystical enclosure that had housed and protected many of China's emperors.

Several large parks existed within the walls and outside the walls. Pei Hai was, and continues to be a beautiful, large lake within the walls where we ice-skated in winter when the lake froze. At one end of the lake was a delicate garden built for one of the Empresses as a gift from her son. Plants and reflecting ponds with brightly colored carp and sculpted jade statues could be seen beneath the water. Narrow pathways circled the garden on which people strolled quietly soaking up the peacefulness of the surroundings.

The Temple of Heaven was an elaborate structure formed in a perfect circle. Nearby was the famous "whispering wall", an acoustic phenomenon. If a person stood on one side of the wall and whispered, a person standing several feet away, diagonally to the other side of the circular wall, could hear the whisper.

Further from the walled city were places like the Summer Palace Shrine with moored marble boats, the Jade Fountain—another fabulous shrine and park, the Temple of the Four Hundred Sleeping Gods and the Imperial Hunting Grounds. Beyond all these were the famous Ming Tombs which led the way to the Great Wall of China.

As I picture myself visiting those incredible, historic masterpieces that I was seeing for the first time, I remember being impressed by their uniqueness, but I do not remember being moved by their beauty. Fact was more important than "fancy" and the facts were I considered the Chinese an impoverished peasant society of no great importance in 1946.

Not only was the weather in Peking extreme at times, with scorching summers and freezing winters, several times a year there arose sand storms that blew in from the Mongolian Gobi desert. One could forecast when such a storm would hit. The distant western sky would start turning a grayish brown. There would be sudden gusts of wind swirling the leaves around in the streets and gradually increasing in strength. Slowly, bits of sand filled the air. The city would shut down. People shuttered their houses, shops closed, and precautions were taken to minimize the damage of the impending storm. And finally the sand would hit with ferocious force. If one got caught in the street wearing heavy winter attire and facing away from the storm, the sand hit one's trousers so hard that the sting was unbearable. The aftermath of such a storm left the city like the Gobi Desert itself—sand was everywhere despite the precautions. Houses, buildings, stores would be full of the fine grit. It took days for the city to return to normal.

Our AMP group was billeted in barracks that had once belonged to the Austrian Legation. The barracks were constructed of several brick single storied buildings. These were an engineering feat as far as temperature control was concerned. In summer, when it was unbearably hot, the buildings stayed cool. In freezing winters, when the temperature went below zero, a coal burning furnace heated the space between the double layered brick walls and kept the buildings warm. We set up an office for operations in one of the buildings, requisitioning necessary vehicles for our security duties, arranged for our own mess, and got everything in working order.

Capt. Hussey and I had to work closely together to run our outfit and he pretty much relied on me because of his lack of experience in China. He could not pronounce my family name, so he called me "Bush". Being from Arkansas he loved hot and spicy food. The twenty five Indians and Pakistanis (ex-policemen from Shanghai) guarded a huge ammunition dump about twenty five miles from Peking. These people were hired specifically for this job. No one else would take it. It was too dangerous. They had their own living quarters and mess hall within the dump. Because of their different religions, there was a problem with the food—the Sikhs could not eat beef and the Moslems could not eat pork. They solved this very amicably. Six days a week, they had common acceptable fare—lamb, chicken, fish, etc. On Thursdays, they split. The Sikhs would have pork and the Moslems would have beef. The Thursday menu was heavy on curries—almost exclusively.

Capt. Hussey had to check out the ammunition depot often. He did not want to go alone, so he would drag me along. He would time these trips close to noon, so he could have his hot curries. Very often, he would choose Thursdays. You know why? He knew I hated the curry.

After lunch on our drive back to Peking in a Jeep, he greatly enjoyed seeing me with my mouth wide open trying to cool off the hot curry taste. However, after some time, I got used to the hot meals to the point of loving it as much as Captain Hussy. The hotter the better!

I had been working in Peking for a few months when a young GI suddenly appeared in our midst. He was very pleasant and friendly especially to the Russian AMPs. He would stop by our barracks after five o'clock and hang around talking to the men. We suspected that he was undercover, and possibly spoke Russian. One evening, when we were alone enjoying a few drinks, he asked me if I would ever consider working for U.S. Intelligence. I was both surprised and flattered, but part of me doubted he was serious. He told me to think it over. He did not need an immediate answer. I fantasized a bit about being an undercover agent. Some time later, when we were again alone, he again broached the subject.

This time I knew he was not joking. I asked him what would be involved. He said I would undergo intense training and then be dropped into the Soviet Union by parachute as an underground operative. He told me everything would be taken care of behind the Iron Curtain. I thought to myself, "I take chances, but this is a bit over the top, even for me." I told him I would perhaps consider this proposition on the condition I be guaranteed that my parents and sister would be allowed to immigrate to the U.S. He said he would get back to me with an answer. I never received a response. Shortly thereafter, he disappeared. We later learned that he was not a G.I. He was an officer in a covert military intelligence unit.

As I stated previously, all the Allied nations were hoping for the creation of a coalition government between General Chiang Kai Shek's forces and those of Mao's Communist forces. It was never going to work. Mao was gaining both strength and followers, mostly from the peasants who had suffered for generations from neglect and abuse. Chiang Kai Shek, who started out as a patriot, was weakening at a fast rate. He was considered, with good reason, to be corrupt by almost everyone, including the Americans and me. His wife was also widely rumored to be a major contributing factor to his corruption. It wasn't surprising that Mao, with the help of the Soviet Union, was successfully regrouping in Manchuria, to begin his offensive southward. Chiang Kai Shek was in retreat. Towards the end of summer of 1947, the Communist armies controlled all of China north of Peking and there were many pockets of communist partisans south of Peking.

Land routes in and out of Peking became unsafe. Trucks were either robbed or hijacked by partisans.

The trains, even though they were heavily guarded by Chiang's troops, were not always safe for cargo transport or for travelers. When the U.S. Peking Headquarters Command slowly began its withdrawal in mid 1947, U.S. military air transports were the only secure mode of transportation. All remaining American forces, their families, support staff like Walter and me, and all other AMPs waited for their air transports out of Peking.

It was part of our contract with the U.S. Army that all of the workers from Shanghai would be returned there. There was a gradual reduction of our group and by mid summer of 1947 there were only a handful of us left on security duty. The city was being choked by the communist partisans. One of our AMP drivers, while changing guards for the midnight shift, left his vehicle to walk a short distance to the post. When he returned with the replacement guard, the vehicle was gone. None of these military vehicles had keys. One just had to flip a switch and drive, so they were very easy to steal. The U.S. military suspected that this incident might involve the AMP people. Our departure dates to Shanghai were held up pending investigation of the stolen vehicle. The very next day in broad daylight, a Jeep used by an American lieutenant was stolen. The following day, again in broad daylight, two more vehicles driven by U.S. officers were stolen. In spite of strict orders not to leave motorized transports unattended, they continued to be stolen. It was evident it was the work of the communists who needed all the equipment they could get to aid in the fight against Chiang Kai Shek's retreating forces. The thefts of U.S. military cars and trucks continued. We were naturally not pleased with our departure date being delayed and we went to the U.S. military authorities. After we presented our case to the very same captain that suspected us in the first place, he simply scratched his head and said our travel orders to Shanghai would be ready the next day. A few days later, along with the many U.S. personnel, we boarded the second last MATS (Military Air Transport Service) plane out of Peking to Shanghai. After the last MATS plane left, only fighter planes remained.

⁓◈⁓

Back in Shanghai

Our jobs with the Army finished, Walter and I had big ideas about our future in Shanghai. No more lowly jobs for us. We would get jobs with an import/export firm and wear a suit and tie and make some money. We arrived in Shanghai in early fall of 1947. Our old room at Colonel Apreleff's house had been rented out. We picked up our belongings and moved to another rooming house. The Shanghai we had left just a short time ago had all but disappeared. The people of Shanghai were caught in the immense struggle that was facing all of China: the fight for power between Mao and Chiang Kai Shek. The busy, bustling city, ready to do business right after the war, was slowly closing down. Shops were gradually empty-ing, foreign businessmen were leaving at a rapid rate and Walter and I had to rethink our very ambitious plans. Companies were firing not hiring. And so with a heavy and definitely humble heart we again went to the U.S. Army in Shanghai for a job. Even the Army was not hiring many people, but they were interviewing for a typing position. There were eight applicants, seven girls and me. I got the job and at least had some income. Walter was not so lucky.

Working for the army, a job with no future was not what I had in mind. It is a wonder that I, not known for being calm or patient, accepted my present state only as a temporary set back. A couple of months passed and I received word, that after several attempts by my parents, permission for me to enter Japan was finally granted by the Occupation Forces in Japan "for compassionate reasons". My one concern was for my friend, Walter. I was the one with the job, but by some miracle, he had a position lined up at the U.S. Army motor pool, so my conscience was clear. I booked passage on American President Lines and left Shanghai. No more Army, typing, or olive green uniforms. I was confident that the future would be better. Home was a few days away and my family was waiting for me. The war had taken six long years of our lives during which the happy-go-lucky boy they had known had changed.

❧❧

RETURN TO JAPAN—1947

The ship that took me back to Japan was an American President Lines troop ship with a few individual staterooms for officers and VIP's, but the rest of the accommodations were large sleeping quarters consisting of several stacked bunks. This was the only type of ship available at the time. On board were many passengers who were going to America and had to share accommodations with people like me. The ship's first port of call was my disembarkation point, Yokohama, Tokyo's port. While I had written to my parents about my arrival, I also cabled them from the ship informing them the exact time of my arrival. As I neared Yokohama, my excitement mounted at the thought of seeing my family once more.

When we were docking, I looked down at the pier from the deck and it appeared to be unchanged. There was no evidence of the destruction that I expected to see. When I enquired about this to a young American naval officer who happened to be on deck with me, he told me that the allies purposely did not target the port and its environs so it could be used once the war was won just as they had done in Shanghai. I walked down the gangplank with my meager baggage, glad to feel solid ground under my feet.

Looking around for my family I noticed the Allied military everywhere, but no family to greet me. I waited a while and still no shouts of welcome. Getting nervous I was disappointed and a bit peeved. I walked over to the small military police check point, explained my predicament, and asked to use the telephone. Luckily my parents were one of the privileged few to acquire a telephone, no easy feat at that time. My mother answered, totally surprised, and asked "Where are you?" "I'm at the dock in Yokohama waiting to be picked up! Didn't you get my wire?" I responded rather impatiently.

My mother said they received no wire, but she would send my sister to pick me up. It was Saturday and my sister was not at work. I went outside the check point and sat on my suitcase. Before long, a Jeep driven by a Japanese employee of the U.S. Forces with a pretty blond girl sitting beside him, pulled up next to me and screeched to a stop. It had been three years since I had seen or heard her voice. My sister was now a full fledged woman. She jumped out of the Jeep. Her laugh was the same. I could not help but think "All we have been through and she is still Lala." What a relief it was to see that she had not changed. At least on the outside. I don't know what I would have done if the war had made the sister I knew disappear like so much of my life. We hugged each other and kissed on both cheeks. I grabbed my bags, threw them into the back of the Jeep and away we went.

The untouched harbor of Yokohama faded from view as the landscape of the bombed-out city of Yokohama appeared in its stark devastation. There was not much debris, but shattered shells of buildings were lined up liked skeletons. We passed a few civilian automobiles as we drove on newly paved roads. Most of the motor traffic was due to the Occupation Force vehicles. Only a few automobiles and trucks were driven by the local Japanese. Almost all Japanese vehicles that survived the war were fueled by gas produced by charcoal burners mounted in their trunks. In the city I noted the contrast of the people who once were so confident and optimistic and now were trying to make do with little. The remnants of their leaders' folly surrounded them. Like most human beings who have suffered terrible losses, the Japanese people were moving on with their lives trying to survive the death of loved ones, the destruction of their homes and possessions, and most of all the extinguishment of their pride.

◈

MY FAMILY'S SURVIVAL JOURNEY

My family's survival journey was very different from my own. I mentioned earlier that as Japan was targeted for constant bombings, women and children were ordered to relocate to the mountains or countryside where it was safer. My sister and mother had rented a small summer house in a mountain resort area at Lake Nojiri, about 150 miles north of Tokyo. Meanwhile, my father was told he had to stay behind in Yokohama to deal with civilian emergency concerns, manning water containers and sand bags in case of bombings by the Americans. By late 1944 the Americans began a gradual heavy bombing of the larger cities. In May of 1945, Yokohama was carpet bombed and our flat was set afire by a nearby explosion. Fortune was with my father, for he was not injured. The Grand Hotel was close to the port and still intact. One of my St. Joseph school friends was the assistant manager there and he helped my father by getting him a room so at least he had a place to sleep and bathe. The next day, because my father lost his home, he was given permission by the Japanese authorities to join my mother and sister in the mountains. That day or the next, he was on a train out of Yokohama.

Although they had money, the rations they received hardly were able to sustain them. My sister traveled on her bicycle over rural roads visiting the houses of local farmers begging to purchase food. "We have only enough for our own family", they all said. It was evident that the Japanese farmers had no need of cash, so my sister changed tactics and asked if they needed any material goods, such as clothing.

My mother, for some reason, stripped all the windows in our house of their drapes which were made of heavy, brown velveteen. Her sewing skills came in handy. She began sewing all kind of garments, especially trousers, in exchange for food. It was not long before many farmers, men as well as women, could be seen wearing very similar outfits. My family now was able to barter for food and provisions they needed to survive. They were kept alive, but by the war's end they were all very thin. My father, who had been a sturdy two hundred-pounder, lost fifty pounds. Both my mother and sister also were underweight.

When they returned to the charred city of Tokyo, after the war ended, they did not know whether I was dead or alive in China. My sister still speaks of that terrible time as one of the worse experiences of her life. Because Shanghai was not a target of bombing raids, my parents did not have the same fear that I had about their survival. It was assumed that I was alive, but they could not be sure and they could not get any information about me. The Post Office in Japan served only Japanese residents. The American military was the only source of mail outside the country in those days. It was when my sister began to work for the U.S. forces that she was able to contact the Red Cross who, with the help of the American Occupational Forces, found me. "When we received word you were alive and well, Ma started to weep and Pa got out the vodka!", my sister told me. "Pa said he knew you were okay and we all raised our glasses! Nazdarovia! (to Health!)".

While in Nojiri, nearby to my family's house, lived a young Bulgarian woman named Zika Maeda, with two small children, a boy and girl. Before Pearl Harbor her husband, Mr. Maeda, had been a roving journalist for a Japanese news agency covering Europe. He was in Bulgaria in 1941 when he met Zika. After a very short courtship, they eloped and left for Tokyo.

A few years after the Pacific War started Mrs. Maeda relocated to Nojiri, while her husband was forced to stay in Tokyo. Russian and Bulgarian being similar languages, my family, especially my mother, became very close friends with Zika. My family was a great help to her, which she and her husband appreciated since her Japanese was weak. This friendship continued after both families returned to Tokyo.

The love story of Zika and Mr. Maeda was not typical in those days when east and west were clearly delineated. It took courage to marry an outsider in both cultures. Their marriage lasted until the untimely death of Zika. Mr. Maeda had advanced in his career to being the president of the largest broadcasting company, N.H.K., in Japan. I remember attending Nika's funeral at the Russian Orthodox church in Tokyo after the war. Limousines lined the streets causing traffic to stop. It was an impressive tribute to a beautiful, kind and adventurous woman and to her husband who loved her dearly.

∾∿

GENERAL MACARTHUR AND THE BIRTH OF A NEW JAPAN

If a perfect leader was to be found, Japan could not have been more fortunate in the appointment of General Douglas MacArthur as Supreme Commander of the Allied Forces in the Pacific (generally referred as SCAP). In every era there seems to be a few extraordinary persons with qualities necessary to be truly heroic in stature. General MacArthur was such a figure. He was ramrod straight in posture, classically handsome, imperious in attitude and oozing superiority. MacArthur not only commanded the Allied Forces in the Pacific, his presence dominated wherever he chose to be. I saw him many times in Tokyo. Accompanied by aides and other support staff, he never appeared to be in a hurry. Because of his outward appearance and charisma he attracted the attention he expected and obviously enjoyed. He understood the culture of the Japanese people and respected it. He also understood the need to be the personification of America's superiority and power. He set about establishing the rules he demanded to be obeyed without exception. There was to be no denigrating or humiliation of the Emperor. He allowed the Japanese administrators who were in place to continue to manage cities and towns with American oversight. The war mongers and militarists were purged, convicted and punished. Some were executed after lengthy trials.

The Americans tried very hard to alleviate hunger and to supply necessary medical facilities to the citizens of Japan. In general, the Japanese accepted the occupation as unavoidable and with stoic acquiescence. They didn't like foreigners in their country, but I saw no outward signs of hatred toward the Americans who were generous and non-confrontational with the populace. Everyone was tired of everything having to do with war and wanted to begin again. As did I. I had no money, no job and the adjustment of living as a family again was not easy. We all had been changed. The war had taken its toll on all of us.

❧❧

THE NEED FOR ENTERTAINMENT

In an occupied country with military personnel everywhere, one commonality is the desire for entertainment. There were clubs for officers of the occupational forces, clubs for the noncoms and for common soldiers. There were also Japanese entertainment establishments in Tokyo that catered to the local clientele.

The traditional Japanese bar was different from its American counterparts. If one went to a shop and purchased a bottle of Japanese beer, it would cost about thirty or forty cents. When an American soldier went to a Japanese bar or club, the beer would cost $1.50. Of course, the soldier was also able to enjoy the company of a hostess and being served by a bartender at a table, but the difference in price did not seem fair to many American GI's. They thought they were being cheated. It was not unusual for arguments or even fights to erupt over this perceived injustice. Eventually, in order to avoid these disturbances, it was unofficially agreed, by both Japanese club owners and the Allied officials, to make many of these Japanese establishments "off limits" to all military personnel.

One would think that with all these different bars, saloons and clubs, there were enough places for everyone to enjoy themselves over a beer or two, but there was one group that was without a proper venue for relaxing. Non-Japanese businessmen, foreign diplomatic people and others were slowly arriving in Japan. Although they could be a guest at any of the military clubs, they could not go on their own.

Enter Mr. Edouard Gordes, another former St. Joseph classmate. His grandfather, a Frenchman, had come to Japan in the late 1800's or early 1900's to Nagasaki to establish the first bakery in Japan. To this day the Japanese word for bread is "pan", the French word for bread, although it is spelled differently. Eddie was a quarter French, but he looked more Japanese than European. He was assistant manager of the prestigious Imperial Hotel during the war because of his knowledge of languages. When the war ended, he remained as assistant manager under the Occupation Forces. This hotel was used exclusively by Allied officers traveling back and forth from many different areas in the Pacific.

Eddie Gordes and a Japanese entrepreneur approached me with an idea to open a foreigner's club. A person like me with a western face was deemed more appropriate to apply for the necessary permits from the Japanese authorities to open such a club. I still did not have a job and I was living with my parents. I had room and board, but I needed to find work. So I agreed to be their front person and help bring their idea to fruition. All three of us went to the necessary Japanese government offices to apply for all the permits needed to begin the project. Speaking Japanese as a native and having a foreigner's face was the right combination to obtain the permits.

Before long, the Tokyo Foreigners' Club opened for business with me as manager. I was finally earning a comfortable salary in Yen and wearing a suit and necktie.

The Tokyo Foreigners' Club was created to fit western tastes. The building was modest, but the location was close to the center of the city with many fine restaurants nearby. The club had a small bar with one bartender. Instead of bistro tables, there were comfortable sofas and chairs, creating an atmosphere not unlike an exclusive men's club. We were open only in the evening. Hostesses, so important in Japanese clubs, were not part of the ambience, although there were two waitresses. Food was kept to an assortment of filling snacks. Initiation fees and monthly dues were kept low to encourage enrollment. Drinks and food were also very affordable.

During the next few months, the club was quite successful, appealing to a variety of patrons. Non-occupation foreign residents of Tokyo were now able to enjoy themselves as well as entertain their friends and clients. Businessmen who were new to Tokyo now had a pleasant place to relax and meet people. My job was to greet and chat with our members and oversee the daily activities.

One evening, while mingling with members of the club, a fellow came in whom I hadn't seen in years. Eric Crane was his name. He had been a schoolmate about four or five class years ahead of me. Because St. Joseph's was such a small school, we all knew each other. We got reacquainted. Eric, who was half English and half Japanese, told me that he and his family had returned to England before the hostilities began, and he had been drafted into the British army. He rose to the rank of major and saw action in India and Burma. He was now back in Japan.

Crane was a tall, big, muscular guy, with a hoarse voice caused from a fair amount of cigarettes and booze. During the war, he had served under Colonel Brown, a British officer, in the Burma campaign. Colonel Brown's family was the owner of the prestigious trading company in London—Brown MacFarlane & Co., Ltd., that had offices in Japan before the war. Crane had been hired to re-open Brown MacFarlane and manage the office in Tokyo.

One evening at the club, as I was passing by his table, Crane stopped me and asked, "How can I join this club?" "Just pay the initiation fee and you're in." I answered. Later on in the evening, he called me over and asked, "What are you doing here?" It was clear what he really was asking was, "What are you doing in a place like this"?

Half-jokingly, I said, "Find me a better job and I'll take it".

The next day, Eric Crane phoned me with an offer of a job as his much-needed assistant. I gratefully accepted the offer after negotiating my salary. I insisted on being paid in U.S. backed script, with the same buying power as U.S. dollars. The use of American currency was outlawed by American and Japanese governing establishments for a variety of solid reasons such as differing rates of foreign exchange and black marketing of goods that could be purchased at the military PXs with dollars and then sold to the Japanese populace. With the script I was now able to shop in stores set up for non-military and non-Japanese people. These special stores were similar to the U.S. military commissaries. All kind of goods and necessities that were not available on the Japanese market could be purchased there. I was on my way at last! I had a real job that paid decent money, and most of all I had a future.

≈≈≈

1948—LEARNING THE IMPORT/ EXPORT BUSINESS

In September of 1948 I began working as Crane's assistant manager for Brown MacFarlane, an international trading company of fine repute. The British term, trading company, is what Americans refer to as an import/export company. Before the war, Brown MacFarlane traded in cotton goods from Japan to India, wattle bark (a tanning agent) from South Africa to Japan, "momi" (a very light white wood used for packing tea) from Japan to India and quite a few other products and commodities. My job was not like anything I had ever attempted or studied. My only three assets were #1, I could speak Japanese and English, #2, I was pretty good with numbers and #3, I could type. Another hidden asset was my unwavering ambition to succeed. Curious by nature, learning a new business was a welcome challenge. As assistant manager, I made no decisions, but quickly learned how decisions were made.

Mr. Brown, the former Colonel, was a lanky, upper class Englishman with sparse, sandy hair streaked with grey. He was in his mid or late forties with rather florid skin not caused from outdoor activities, but by frequent imbibing of good whiskey. Through his long, thin aristocratic nose emerged a voice with an accent cultivated by years of proper British schooling. Mr. Brown's gestures and manner of speaking were less than masculine which was in direct contrast to the rough and tough Eric Crane.

After work Eric and I would sometimes have a drink together and I once asked him if Mr. Brown really fought on the front lines during the war. "He not only was a brave and courageous soldier, he was a strong officer and leader in battle." Eric answered. "You might say he had some odd, personal quirks. He always carried a black umbrella on marches. If it rained, he led his troops with his umbrella unfurled to protect him from the drops, just as he would in London." It was obvious Eric held the man in high esteem despite his unusual demeanor.

Business slowly started to boom. The Japanese were eager to export their products and get back on their feet. When I think of the way we communicated with customers and suppliers in those days, I marvel at how far the world has come, thanks to technology. The wireless was a miracle back then. It was very expensive to wire long messages, so codes were developed to shorten the procedure. The idea was fine, but there was more than one code system. One of my jobs was to send coded messages to our London office and to other countries where we had clients, and then decode their responses. It was tedious work. Adding to this was the fact that all these messages had to go through the wireless office. We had runners who would take all the communiqués to the wireless office and bring back incoming replies which had to be decoded. It makes me tired just remembering all that movement.

❧❧

FAMILY LIFE RETURNS

The last several years of hardship behind us, we finally adjusted to living happily as a family once again. And
three of us were making money. My sister had a job, I
was working at the British firm, and my father had slowly
resumed his business. We were able to buy a used car, a
Hudson sedan, from a U.S. colonel. In the beginning of
the occupation, Japanese and non-military persons could
not buy vehicles from the occupational forces. Some time
later, cars could be purchased, but only with U.S. dollars
or scrip.

Considering the scarcity of housing, not only in
Tokyo, but in all large cities, the small house we were
fortunate to rent was adequate, but we could now afford to improve our lot and we did. There were many
skilled construction workers available who were anxious
for work. Their wages were low due to the competition.
Count Asano, a member of an old Japanese family, owned
about two acres of prime residential property in central

Tokyo that he was forced to sell to settle his tax debts. We purchased a quarter acre corner lot from him. Two sides of the lot bordered streets and the other two sides abutted two Japanese houses. We proceeded to build our new home with the best materials available at that time. We moved in at the close of 1949. The house had two stories and was western in design. Downstairs consisted of the living room, dining room, kitchen with an adjoining maid's room, one bedroom and a large bathroom. We had hot water, flush toilets, a sewage system and all the necessary conveniences. Upstairs there were two more bedrooms. We had a fairly large garden in the front of the house. We rarely saw the neighbor in the back of our house because of the high fence between us. The other neighbor to the side, with a low bamboo trellis-like fence, was occupied by an amiable retired Japanese insurance man and his wife. The man's passion was growing dahlias that we could see from our house.

During construction, the workers had built a shed of sorts on the side of the lot where they lived while they were building the house. We kept that shed for storage and added a small carport. We were very happy in our new home and pleased to be living a comfortable life once more.

Soon after I started working for Brown MacFarlane, I was introduced to hunting by an American civilian working for the U.S. Forces. He was from New Mexico and he would plead with me to go with him. He would supply all the necessary gear. The reason he insisted I accompany him was again—language. In the good hunting areas, which were quite distant from Tokyo, nobody spoke English. I helped him in arranging lodgings and hiring hunting guides. Japan did not have game hunting as such, but birds were plentiful—ducks, some geese, golden pheasants, quail, doves. Hunting at this time was not a popular sport with the Japanese. I started liking the sport and soon acquired my own gear. We usually tried to stay in hot springs areas, where after hunting all day, it was relaxing and invigorating to soak in the hot tub or pool.

In some of the larger inns, where the hot spring tubs or pools were communal, men and women soaked "au naturel". Hot spring bathing was considered very healthful and therapeutic. Even though men and women bathed naked together, it was done with the utmost reserve and decorum.

᠊ᢙᠵᢙ᠊

Fun Begins

One afternoon, some time after I started working for Brown MacFarlane, as I was riding down in an elevator in an undamaged office building in central Tokyo, I thought I recognized a Japanese gentleman who had been a mild acquaintance of mine in Shanghai. I got to know him because he lived in the French Concession in an apartment complex where one of my Aurora University classmates resided. At that time, he was engaged in procurement—I'm not sure of what—for the Japanese government. Because I spoke Japanese, we occasionally spoke to each other.

When he got off the elevator, I followed him and tapped him lightly on his shoulder. "Mr. Shimizu"? I asked. He turned around and recognized me. He told me he was now engaged in import/export trade with Korea. We had a short visit, exchanged name cards, and decided to meet some evening after work.

Before long, we met for a drink at a posh, intimate night club of his choosing. The world of sleek sophistication was new to me and I loved the excitement. I had some money, I was free of personal commitments, and I had a myriad of bad times to erase. Let the good times begin! And begin they did.

A great advantage in attracting girls was speaking Japanese like a native. At that time Japanese girls were anxious to meet foreigners. Mr. Shimizu and I would go to a night club and he would order drinks. There were always attractive hostesses in clubs to entertain customers. Mr. Shimizu would begin the conversation in Japanese, but speak to me in English. The girls would giggle not knowing I spoke their language. Often they would make fun of my long nose, at the instigation of Mr. Shimizu. There is an old Japanese joke that compares the length of a man's nose to the size of another part of a man's anatomy. That joke was told many times. After a while, I would get up, and ask in Japanese where the "Chozuba" was, an archaic and seldom used word for toilet. They always did a "double-take" then laugh and laugh. Speaking of noses, as a western man my nose is long compared with the short noses of the Japanese people. Often the girls would admire my European nose. "No, no. You have just the right size nose." I would say. "If I try to kiss a western girl with a nose like mine our noses bump each other! Do you know what I have to do? I have to bend my nose to reach their lips." I would demonstrate by pulling my nose to one side in a comic way. Let me say that these little performances worked wonders on those pretty girls and opened many doors. It was loads of fun and continued to be so for some time.

Not only were night club hostesses anxious to meet Western men, girls from good families, girls working in offices, stores and other places, were just as anxious. Before I met Mr. Shimizu I went out with many Japanese girls that I met through mutual friends. There were some European and American girls living or working in Tokyo, but I, and others like me, were not in a position to meet or date them because there was an established social structure.

The social structure went something like this: Occupation Forces came to Japan first. About the same time came the Department of Army Civilians (DACs), who were men and women hired in the U.S. as support staff to the Occupation Forces. Then many wives and children followed. All these people socialized together. They had their own housing, schools, clubs, movies, etc. Fraternizing was just not done.

As I stated, there were very few opportunities for me to meet non-Japanese girls. And to be honest, I really was not interested. The Japanese girls that I was meeting through mutual friends and in night clubs were easy to be with. I was not in a position to form lasting attachments. I did not consider it an option for me to marry a Japanese girl. Having seen how difficult it was for many of my St. Joseph's schoolmates who were the products of mixed-marriages, I wanted to avoid that fate for any children I may have. But most of all was my desire to go to the United States unattached and with no responsibilities.

There was an attractive, well educated Japanese girl whose father was a prominent publisher and distributor of Japanese and foreign magazines in Osaka who happened to be a good friend of Mr. Maeda, (the same Mr. Maeda whose wife, Zika, had been a friend of my mother in Lake Nojiri). I met the young lady through Mrs. Maeda, who enjoyed playing the role of matchmaker. This girl came to Tokyo often to visit friends. I was being pressured to invite the girl out and finally I agreed to Mrs. Maeda's urging and invited the girl to dinner. We enjoyed each other's company. The next time she came to Tokyo, she called me just to say hello and I invited her out again.

During the next few months, we got together occasionally when she came to Tokyo. One evening, after a leisurely dinner, I drove her to her friend's house where she was staying. Before she went in, we sat in the car and talked about inconsequential things, but the conversation developed into a more serious vein. I shared with her my long held dream of emigrating to the U.S. and in order to do that, it was my choice to remain single.

There was silence. The silence continued, and I looked at her and saw that she was crying softly. I was surprised and asked her what was wrong. She did not respond until she controlled her tears. "It would be best if we did not see each other again", she finally said. I thought to myself, "What is this all about?" and tried to embrace her saying I was sorry. She pulled way from me and said she had better go in now. I took her to the front door and kissed her goodbye.

As I drove home, I thought to myself, did she think we that we might marry? We kissed a few times, but we were never intimate. I never meant to hurt her.

I came to understand the circumstances in which young Japanese women found themselves. So many young Japanese men were killed in the war. Who were these girls going to marry? Marriage was the most important part of woman's life at that time. No wonder every single man was so popular. From then on, I realized I had to be careful in my relationships with Japanese girls. I later heard that this nice girl went to the U.S. to attend a university. I never saw her again.

✌✍

MY OWN BUSINESS

Brown MacFarlane was doing well. I was getting experience and knowledge in all aspects of the import/export business, such as how to deal with manufacturers, pricing, the language of the trade, what all the initials stood for (FOB meant free on board, CIF meant cost insurance freight, on and on). As the first year, then the second passed, I became more and more eager to start my own company. It never occurred to me that I could fail.

My friend, Mr. Shimizu, introduced me to a Mr. Takagi, who was from a well-to-do family that owned a building close to General MacArthur's headquarters. A small space with two desks became available. The war had destroyed many of the commercial buildings in Tokyo and office space was so scarce it was common practice to share accommodations. I was fortunate to get those two desks and a bit of space that would house the start-up company with Mr. Takagi, soon to be known as Konwal Trading Company. The "Kon" was me and the "wal" was for my old Shanghai friend and roommate, Walter. I had made a pact with my friend many years ago that we would name our company with a combination of both of our names. I felt I had to keep that promise even though he had immigrated to Australia and our partnership was not to be.

Needing the steady income, I continued to work for Brown MacFarlane. I worked early morning, evenings and weekends at my company while Mr. Takagi managed the business during the day. I paid all the bills. His job was to get as much information as possible from the Tokyo Chamber of Commerce which had the names of all international prospective customers searching for products and goods. Japan was anxious to resume the trade it had enjoyed before the war. Inquiries came from all over the world and the Chamber would itemize those inquiries for people like us to read. Before long we hit the jackpot. From a list of companies wanting Japanese goods we learned that a firm in India was looking for ball-bearings. Mr. Takagi contacted a large manufacturer of these goods, and we made the offer to the Indian firm. We got the order, eventually received the necessary letter of credit from India and made all the arrangements needed for shipping. My lucky day turned out to be Friday the 13th of July, 1950. Eventually I left Brown MacFarlane, as my own business slowly got going.

Around this time, I ran into another schoolmate from St. Joseph's with whom I had been friendly and who was working for the U.S. Army commissary in Northern Japan. The base had closed and he had returned to Tokyo. After several meetings he agreed to work for me as a minor partner. He was half Japanese and half Estonian, tall and very European looking. When the Korean War started, the United Nations forces, which consisted primarily of the U.S. military, started buying war related merchandise such as bomb casings, tires, and some spare machine parts that could be delivered on short notice where needed as well as household items like paint brushes. The U.S. buying agency was open for bids on items they needed. We made some offers and got a few small orders for paint brushes and coffee mugs. We offered cigarette lighters that were being made at the time, but the lighters did not sell because of the poor quality.

Zippo cigarette lighters were the most popular at the time. I decided to try to make a Zippo type lighter that matched the quality of the U.S. brand. Zippo's patent had long expired. At the PXs, a Zippo sold for $1.25. We approached a manufacturer of lighters and discussed producing a quality product. They were negative on the idea saying it would not sell. At this stage the Japanese emphasis was not on quality, but on price. I told them I wanted them to produce a prototype that could be tested for quality. They agreed to produce two hundred lighters using the best materials available. This experiment was costly and a big gamble for my company. We offered the newly manufactured lighters to the U.S. military buying agency for fifty-five cents apiece. We had a nice profit margin for ourselves. The buying agency had these lighters tested with an accredited American testing company stationed in Japan. The verdict was that our lighters "were as good, if not better than Zippos". To our great surprise, we got an order for ninety-six thousand pieces! The gamble paid off.

We phoned the manufacturers who had been anticipating some kind of an order. At their invitation, we met with the president and vice president of the firm in a posh restaurant of their choosing. They expected us to negotiate their price downward, as was customary. We told them we would give them an order on one condition— that they would absolutely and unconditionally guarantee the quality of each and every lighter. If they agreed to this condition, we would add an extra 10.00 Yen to their original asking price. You should have seen the expression on the faces of these two Japanese men. They were surprised that I was offering them a higher price, instead of trying to negotiate a lower one. We received constant orders for these lighters under our brand "Konwal" which was stamped on the bottom of every lighter.

Due to the uneven distribution of these lighters in the PXs in Korea, they were not always available at some of the PXs on a regular basis. One day, unexpectedly, some Turkish soldiers who had fought with the U.N. forces, came to our office in Tokyo after they were discharged wanting to buy our lighters before returning home. How they found our office was a mystery. We explained that we were not authorized to sell to them. They were surprised and elated when we gave each of them a dozen free of charge. They deserved to get a break.

Another interesting deal we had during the Korean War was obtaining toys for a U.S. chaplain who was in charge of several orphanages in Korea. A month or so before Christmas, he would fly in with an empty cargo plane to buy toys for the orphaned kids of Korea. We were asked by the U.S. buying agency to accommodate him. We would contact as many toy makers as possible and usually were able to buy their overloaded inventory and unsold lots at a good discount. It took a lot of time and physical labor to fill that cargo plane with thousands of toys. We were exhausted, but the chaplain was ecstatic.

The toy manufacturers were happy because it was an unexpected windfall for them. Their happiness was two fold. Japanese tradition required that all households, businesses and establishments had to begin the New Year totally "clean". They would stay up late cleaning their homes until they were spotless. The same would hold true for their businesses. They paid their debts, sold as much of their stock as possible and cleaned the premises. Government and bureaucrats updated and cleared up their unfinished business. On New Year's Day, everybody rested, celebrated and looked forward to a prosperous future. Celebrations usually lasted up to a whole week.

The chaplain was happy, the children would have toys, the toy makers were happy and we joined in.

ومهمو

AND THEN THERE WAS ONE

Post-war Japan was teeming with American service men. My sister, Lala, as I have described her, was a fun-loving blond. She spoke perfect English and was very popular with the American servicemen so far from home, constantly being invited to dinners, movies and dances. Quite a few servicemen, both officers and GI's visited our home. Among her many admirers was a young, handsome sergeant named Bill Logan, who was the most persistent. When she agreed to marry him, she insisted it had to be kept secret. My father was very strict and old-fashioned. When my parents found out about the marriage they were less than pleased. It took some time, but finally all was forgiven just before the sergeant was transferred to Great Falls, Montana. Naturally my sister went with him. I can tell you Lala was a city girl and the marriage did not last long in the wide open spaces of Montana. They were soon divorced and she decided to move to San Francisco. That decision would impact all of the Balabushkins.

By the early 1950s the Cold War was heating up. The Soviet Union was not allowing their citizens to leave or emigrate. At that time, U.S. immigration was based on a quota system allowing a certain number of people into the U.S. from various countries. It was based on one's place of birth, whether you were a citizen of that country or not. Since Soviet citizens were not allowed to emigrate, the quota for Russians like my parents was wide open. My parents applied for visas. I also applied, but I was under the Chinese quota because of my place of birth. The Chinese quota was crowded with Chinese natives and stateless people like me, trying to escape the new communist regime.

After a short time, my parents received a response that was not at all expected. My father's application was denied. He was deemed "undesirable". Because my father spoke only halting English, it fell upon me to go to the U.S. consulate to find out why he was so labeled.

Upon entering the consulate, I was directed to an officer who was very courteous and I could tell, took his responsibilities seriously. I asked him why my father was branded "undesirable" and was told no reason would be forthcoming. I did not give up. I pressed on. "Could it be that my father had belonged to a ridiculous Russian émigré, fascist-inspired organization for a short time during the war?" I asked. "He quit after attending a few meetings." This was the fascist organization I described earlier composed of mostly White Russian officers who detested the Reds and wanted to go back and fight for Mother

Russia. "My father was never a fascist!" I continued. The officer said nothing. I left the consulate with no information, but got the sense I had touched on the cause.

It was commonly known that the American Occupational Forces had an intelligence section that kept tabs on all foreigners residing in Japan—a branch dealing specifically with those who had lived in Japan before, during, and after the war. A few days later, I decided to go to the C.I.D. (Criminal Investigation Department), a branch of U.S. Military Intelligence that I knew dealt with matters of this kind.

After several tries, I was able to get an appointment with the officer I had happened to meet previously. He was in charge of Russian émigrés. He agreed to see me at a designated spot in Tokyo, not in his office, but in his Jeep. He had been a high ranking officer with the Chicago police department before the war and was now an important Military Intelligence officer in Tokyo. I related my father's story to him. His response was guarded, but hopeful, as he hinted that, in time, my father probably would be allowed to enter the United States. Some time elapsed and my parents re-applied for a visa. Within a year they received a formal letter granting my father and my mother permission to enter the United States.

The senior Balabushkins left for the States in mid 1954 and now I was the only one left in Japan waiting for my visa application to be approved. Alone in a big house, doing rather well in my export and PX business, I had a lot of evenings to fill. With money in my pockets and time on my hands, the combination proved to be danger-ous for a fellow like me. I worked hard all day and spent most evenings bar hopping and night clubbing into the wee hours of the morning.

By then, I was no longer known as Konstantin Poli-carpovich Balabushkin. My nice Slavic name was too long and difficult for the Japanese to pronounce because they have no L sound in their language. My name in the Japanese pronunciation became "Konstanching Barabu-shiking". It also took too much time to sign export docu-ments, seven sets for every shipment my company made. So I decided to shorten my name by deleting the middle part of Balabushkin and creating the name "Balin" and at the same time shortening my first name to "Kon" and de-leting Policarpovich. Wanting the new name to be legal, I went to the District Ward Office to apply for a name change. I was directed to a young clerk who asked me the reason for wanting the change. Here again speaking Japanese facilitated the whole procedure. After my expla-nation, the necessary papers were filled out and within a week I had a new name and a new identity. Kon Balin was born!

✍✍

SEARCHING FOR UNDESIRABLES

The Japanese prized beauty, harmony and serenity, but beneath the surface the underworld bubbled with crime, corruption and immorality. After the war and into the 1950s, the black market, prostitution, gambling and thievery were rampant. Those involved were not limited to the Japanese. A few elements of this corruption were members of the Occupation Forces and other foreign nationals who could not resist the opportunity to make a fast buck.

When Japan signed the peace treaty, the Japanese government formed a national security force to identify and clean out the foreign undesirables. In a very discreet manner, these Japanese security officers began calling on all non-military foreigners residing in Japan. Trying to stem corruption, they continued to keep tabs on all these foreigners.

One day, while I was working in my office, there was a knock on the door and in walked a Japanese man. He handed me his name card with both hands while bowing slightly as is the custom. I read the card and saw he was with the newly formed National Security Force whose responsibility it was to investigate all foreigners in Japan after the peace treaty was signed.

"I am here to introduce myself to you, Mr. Balin. Perhaps you would answer a few questions", he said. I immediately became wary of the fellow. He asked me several questions about my past and was much relieved that I spoke Japanese. After the interview we chatted informally and I told him about my business and mentioned we sold cigarette lighters. I decided it would be to my advantage to make a gift to this man, so I gave him a half dozen.

"Thank you very much." the man said as he started to leave. He turned and said. "I will come back another time." He left the office. "Now what?" I thought. I had nothing to hide, but I didn't like anyone prying into my affairs. He returned several times during the next couple of years to ask me about certain people, some of them had been my schoolmates. I had no information I was willing to share with him. A few of the guys may have been involved in some shady stuff, but who wasn't during the war?

The nosy fellow and I became friendly, so much so that he invited me to tour his headquarters. On one of his last visits I asked him if they had identified all the foreigners they had been looking for. He replied that their task was done, except for one person. They had put in a lot of effort, but were frustrated in their search to find this one person. I asked him who this person was. He replied "Barabushiking". I was surprised, but I grinned and said "I know where he is". He looked stunned in disbelief and asked, "You know him? Where is he"? Again laughingly, I said "You are looking at him". It was then that I informed him that I had changed my name some time ago at the local ward office where I resided. Still somewhat taken aback, he left in a hurry, evidently to check on the veracity of my story. A day or two later, he returned, saying he had checked with the ward office, and that indeed, records showed the facts. He then informed me that the name change was not legal. To change one's name, he said, one must go through the courts. It was not my fault, he acknowledged, it was the clerk's at the ward office. I asked what I should do about it. He said the security people had spent years searching for Mr. Barabushiking and were relieved to have solved the case. "Leave things alone", he said. The security agency would legalize the name change. The man continued to visit, and we would always joke about the missing "foreigner".

❧

AND THEN THERE WAS ONE – CONTINUED

Our European style home was too big for one person. After my parents left for the U.S., the decision was made by the whole family to rent our house. It was rented to a Turkish Consulate's attaché and his family. The rent, while modest, was paid in dollars, which helped my parents in the States. I moved to a newly built studio apartment nearby. Construction of houses and apartments was in full gear at this time. While I was still hopefully waiting for my visa number to come up under the Chinese quota, I kept busy by working hard all day and continued to play hard most of the night. About six months after I had moved out of our house to my small apartment, I received a letter from the American Consulate informing me that my visa application number had finally come up. I was overjoyed! All the years of waiting were soon to end and my dream of living in America was about to come true. Now all I had to do was provide certain documents, the most important of which were sponsorship from the U.S., police records, and a medical report from a U.S. approved doctor.

Having secured all the papers except the medical exam report, I made an appointment with an American doctor at the Seventh Day Adventist hospital in Tokyo who had been approved by the U.S. State Department. The doctor was a kindly man who gave me a thorough examination which included a chest X-ray. When I returned several days later to pick up the report, I was surprised when the doctor asked me to step into his private office. "I can not give you medical clearance." he said. "You have some small spots on the upper part of your left lung." I could not believe what he was saying to me. I wasn't sick. What was he telling me? It must be a horrible mistake! But it was not a mistake, it was true. The doctor told me to return in a month to verify his findings.

I left his office. For a month, that never seemed to end, I tried to go about my life as normally as possible as my fears laid just below the surface. I was filled with anxiety and frustration when I returned to the hospital for the second X-ray. "The spots are still there. You probably have the beginnings of tuberculosis. I can't clear you. I am sorry", said the doctor. Hearing these words was like receiving an unexpected blow. I had to take control of myself in order not to cry. Then I asked him what course I should take. He recommended I enter a sanatorium as soon as possible. The very thought of a sanatorium caused me to experience a kind of panic. The thought of being with all those sick people was abhorrent to me. "I can't do that!" I replied. "Just tell me what I have to do to get well and I'll do it." Reluctantly the doctor outlined a strict regimen for me to follow, warning me that it was my life that was in the balance. I was determined to follow the instructions. As undisciplined as I was about many things, I had always been able to focus on goals that were important to me. Nothing in my life had ever been this important. I was paying for my excesses, not eating well, and not taking care of myself. I caused this disease and I was going to cure it.

Arrangements were made for my partner to take over the management of our business and I went to a mountain resort area called Karuizawa, about ninety miles north of Tokyo to look for a small house to rent. It was early spring. Fortunately, I was able to rent an adequate cottage next to Mikimoto's (of pearl fame) summer house, and hired a local woman who lived nearby to come in daily to cook and take care of the house.

"Eat well, sleep and rest as much as you can" the doctor had said. This might sound like heaven to most people, but to me it was a prescription for Hell! Stuffing my body with food was not something I was going to enjoy. But stuff myself I did—I even ate blood sausage! Doctor's recommendation! At the time I was six feet tall and weighed 145 pounds. The adjustment was brutal. I was extremely lonely and bored. Reading was my only outlet and that got tiresome. Radio was all in Japanese except the U.S. Forces station, which was not always interesting enough for me. The discipline required took every bit of my strength. I hated doing nothing. During the day, while I rested in bed, my feet would constantly twitch out of nervousness. While I used to sleep five or six hours, I began forcing myself to sleep nine to ten hours.

My next appointment with the doctor in Tokyo was to be in forty-five days. The minutes, hours and days passed slowly and finally I was back in Tokyo at the hospital for my third set of x-rays. Even the train ride back to the city was a welcoming respite from boredom.

At the hospital, the x-rays showed no change. That turned out to be good news. The doctor was very pleased that the spots had not grown. "Whatever you're doing, keep it up. And by-the-way, you gained five pounds. That is another good sign", he said smiling. I was to see him in another forty five days.

I went back to the mountains with hope that this nightmare would soon end. I resumed my regimen with renewed vigor and determination. The weather grew warmer and I began to take short walks. It was on one of these walks that I met a man standing by his black motorcycle. We started a conversation and it turned out that he was a physician. He had contracted T.B. while practicing in Tokyo where the air was polluted. He decided to move permanently to Karuizawa to recuperate and devote his medical practice to the treatment of the dreaded disease. I went to see him professionally. He began treating me with a new drug called Hydrazid. He also took x-rays of my lungs and taught me how to read them. I went to see him on a regular basis and we became friendly and saw each other socially on occasion. At least now I had someone to talk to and learn from.

One mild and warm evening I was taking a walk heading towards downtown Karuizawa. Suddenly there was a very loud explosion lifting me off the ground. In front of me the sky turned red followed by dense slate colored smoke. Mt. Asama, some miles from us, had erupted. The eruption ended as quickly as it began leaving the bright glow of reddish orange sweeping across the sky. A fine grey ash descended slowly, settling on everything. It was a startling and frightening event for me, but to those who had lived there all their lives, it was something not unfamiliar, as it occurred about every ten years.

These short vignettes crowd my mind as I remember those days. It is odd how certain images push through the maze and stand there shining.

Another forty-five days passed and again I was back in Tokyo. The x-rays showed evidence of calcifications of the spots on my lungs. I had gained 15 pounds and was finally getting well. The doctor said I was on my way to health. By the end of the summer, I had ballooned up to 220 pounds! I was so fat I could not bend down to tie my shoelaces. I was somewhat worried, but my American doctor assured me that the extra pounds would eventually, if slowly, disappear.

By October, the weather in the mountains was turning cold and I was anxious to return to the city. I received permission from the American doctor to leave the mountains and I rented a small house in the suburbs of Tokyo. A retired Japanese woman, who had worked for Americans, agreed to work for me as a maid/cook. I remember her as a surly type with gold rimmed glasses at the tip of her nose, but she liked the light work the job entailed. Her only pleasure seemed to be going to the movies.

On my later visit to my American doctor in early fall, I pleaded with him to let me go to my office to begin working again. Reluctantly and with admonition, he said I could go one day a week as a start. It was made very clear to me that if I resumed my former way of life, I could get sick again. "Never"! I told myself.

In April of the following year, twelve months after I had begun treatment, I was medically cleared, which meant I could go the U.S., but now there were no visas available—the quotas were all filled. It was likely that the quota would be totaled out for years. The second chance of going to the States had come and gone. The first chance dashed by the war and the second by illness. I found myself giving up hope. Perhaps it was time for me to face the reality that I would never leave Japan, the land in which I had spent so much of my life. My deepest yearnings were again put aside.

By 1955 I was feeling myself again. The doctor was correct. The pounds I had gained in abundance slowly went away, although I did not return to my emaciated 145 pounds. I was back at work full time and had moved back to downtown Tokyo where I rented a room from a widowed Romanian woman, whose house was near the

U.S. Embassy. The two storied house, which had withstood the bombs, was quite large. The Romanian woman lived downstairs. The upstairs, which had a separate entrance, consisted of three bedrooms and a large bathroom. All three bedrooms were rented to single, foreign men. We seldom saw each other. The other two tenants got up early and left for work and returned late at night. I was the last to get up. It worked out conveniently for all three tenants. A few months later, one of the tenants moved, and a new face appeared.

Almost every day I would hear click-click-click coming from across the hall. We had to share the bathroom, so naturally the "clicker" and I met. It turned out he was a writer and the clicking was his typewriter. We were both single and began to have some drinks and of course tell our personal stories. His name was Ronald Kirkbride.

THE STORY OF RONALD KIRKBRIDE
AND THE STORY HE TOLD

Ronald was a great appreciator of women. One day he saw a pretty young Japanese woman entering a bar in the "Ginza" district, one of the largest entertainment centers in Tokyo. She was evidently a hostess. He followed her and tried to enter the establishment, but was stopped by a male employee who told him the place was off-limits to foreigners. Even in the 1950's this policy was still in place. When we met soon after the incident, Ronald asked me if I would go to that bar with him to try to find the girl he had seen. One evening we went there. It was still early and we were the first to enter the place. We went straight to the bar where a young man, with a most unfriendly scowl, was just opening up. Before he could say anything, I ordered two beers in Japanese. To Ronald's astonishment we were served promptly. He was curious why we had no difficulty in entering the place and getting served our drinks. So I asked the bartender in Japanese why my friend was denied entry on another night and tonight we had no trouble. "It's the way you ordered the drinks", he replied. Then the bartender went on to explain that the bars really had no real bias against foreign patrons. They just wanted to avoid trouble with people who did not understand "Japanese ways". After that evening, we would meet for a beer or two and Ronald would ask me a lot of questions about my past. This went on for quite a while. In the meantime, Ronald had met a beautiful, married Japanese woman who was a reception-ist in a downtown hotel. He fell madly in love with her. Her name was Tamiko. He pressured her relentlessly. She eventually left her husband and married Ronald. She had two young children; a boy and a girl, who were both in primary school. Ronald adopted the children. In early 1956, they all left for England and settled in London. He became a successful author. It turned out that one of his most successful novels, "Tamiko", had a protagonist named Ivan Balin whose background was almost a mir-ror image of my own. I was not to find out about this book for many years.

≈ঌৎ≈

YOSHI

Nightclubs were still a draw for me, but now I made sure I ate well, drank sensibly and got enough sleep. While I was driving home one evening, I spotted a girl whose name was Chiyo, crossing the street. She was a hostess at a night club I had often frequented. I stopped to say hello. "I live across the street. I haven't seen you for awhile. Why don't you come up to see my apartment", she said. I parked the car and followed her to the second floor of a modest apartment building. There, in the living room, were three or four girls in informal clothes with curlers in their hair. These girls all shared the same large apartment. When they saw me, I think they were a bit embarrassed because of their appearance and giggled shyly when we were introduced. They were all young with no make-up on their smiling faces. In a short time they would be getting ready for work at an upscale night club called "Ginbasha", meaning "golden horse". We sat and joked with each other for a time. In parting, I said I hoped I would see them sometime at their club.

A few nights later I went to the club. I watched as the hostesses walked in one by one, all in full make-up and wearing glamorous cocktail dresses, placing themselves in a line waiting for the gentlemen clientele to arrive. While I was sitting at the bar, having a beer, I felt a tap on my shoulder. I turned around, and standing there was a tall, striking young woman. Until she spoke, I did not recognize her as one of the girls I had met at Chiyo's apartment. "You look so different. I hardly recognized you." I said. "I am like of ghost when I am working. You met the real me the other day." Yoshi responded. The transformation was truly amazing. I bought her a drink, chatted for a bit and left.

⁂

AND IT BEGAN

It is important to understand that in Japan, women who worked as hostesses were hired to be charming companions to the male patrons of the establishment. Most likely, this modern concept was reminiscent of the geisha tradition which never fully disappeared from Japan. In post-war Japan, with sons, fathers and husbands gone, many young women had to earn money to support their families. Some of the young girls were lucky enough to marry the few eligible men left and live traditional lives, but for many finding work was necessary. Being a hostess in a night club or bar did not mean one was a prostitute. While a few girls extended the idea of "entertainment" to being paid for their sexual favors, most hoped to meet a "sugar daddy" who would keep them in comfort so they could help their families.

One evening, I went to see to see Chiyo at her apartment where she had recently moved. I found that Yoshi had moved into the same newly built apartment complex. Chiyo excused herself to bathe and groom herself for work, and suggested I go to visit Yoshi. I knocked on her door and she let me in. One thing led to another. Yoshi did not go to work that evening.

We liked each other and we slowly fell into a relationship unique to the times. Yoshi and I understood each other. In our own way, we were in love, but we knew, at least I knew, we would never marry.

Born in Nagano prefecture north of Tokyo to a middle class family, Yoshi was the only daughter. Her mother had died when she was in grade school. Her father remarried and had two more daughters. Right after the war ended, she graduated from high school and left for Tokyo to begin a life of her own. She was beautiful, quite tall for a Japanese woman, had an attractive figure, a very cheerful disposition that made her fun to be with. That's why she was employed by one of the best night clubs.

When Yoshi first arrived in Tokyo, there were very few jobs for girls, so she took a job as a maid for an American family. She met a young American GI and they fell in love. She became pregnant. The American boy wanted to marry her, but his family in the States would not allow it. The GI, at the behest of his parents, was sent home. She never saw him again.

Yoshi refused to have an abortion and had the child after the GI went home. She named her little boy Mike, after his father. Her job as a maid did not bring in enough money to support both herself and the childcare she had arranged with a family living in a suburb of Tokyo. That is when she decided to work as a hostess.

As our relationship became more intimate, I asked her if she ever had a child. She was surprised and asked why I asked such a question. I told her I had noticed faint lines on her stomach and hips. She then shared her story about her two year old son. "Would you like to meet him some time?" she asked. "Sure, why not." I replied. A few days later she had Mike brought over to her apartment and I met the little boy – a beautiful child who looked more American than Japanese.

Now, at that time, many childless American couples in Japan were standing in line to adopt children. Yoshi asked me what would be best for her son, whom she loved dearly. She was considering putting him up for adoption. I told her it was her decision, but that it probably would be best for the boy to be adopted. He would have a better chance in the United States than in Japan. It was commonly known that children of mixed heritage were not easily accepted by the Japanese people. The decision was extremely difficult for her, but she finally gave the baby up. He was adopted immediately, and soon left for America with his new mom and dad.

The decision to give up her son was one she grieved over throughout our time together and perhaps throughout her life. Some of her friends had children and it was a constant reminder to her of her own child. Yoshi asked me many times if she did the right thing. I didn't have to answer because she knew in her heart that her little boy would have a better life in America than she could have ever provided for him in Japan.

Yoshi suggested only once that perhaps it would be nice if she moved into my apartment. I said it may be nice, but what would happen if my visa number came up? Where would she be? She understood. We did all kinds of things together like visiting hot springs, going out to dinner and the movies, normal fun things that people do. Under all the intimacy was the unspoken knowledge that we would never marry. One could call it snobbery, or bigotry, but in reality it was just the way it was in 1956, especially in Japan. Our relationship lasted for over two years.

❧❧

Back to Work and a Bit of Play

You might have wondered who was paying my bills while I was in the mountains trying to rid myself of T.B. The business was three-quarters mine. While I was sick my partner drew a salary and I drew a salary from the earnings of Konwal Co. When I returned to work full time, my partner decided he wanted to form his own company in partnership with a Japanese business man. I had no choice but to agree. Then he came to me and wanted his share of the company. During the year of my absence, the business had not prospered because my partner was the kind of person who did what he was hired to do, but no more. He had made no effort to find new customers and was content to collect his salary while filling orders that were contracted before my illness. There were no measurable assets except two cars. In appreciation of his managing the company while I was ill, I told him to take whichever one he wanted and we would call it even.

He left with the best car and I began to concentrate on business once more.

With the departure of my partner, I needed an assistant immediately and began to groom a young employee who had been with Konwal from the start as a messenger. His name was Fumio Tsukamoto, but we called him by his Japanese nickname, Boon. He was only sixteen when he started, and still studying for his high school diploma at night. Boon was very conscientious and eager to learn. If he had free time at work, he would practice typing in English on our portable typewriter. Before long, the typewriter just gave out from all the pounding. We had to buy a new one. We had the old one repaired and told Boon he could type on it all he wanted.

After finishing high school, he continued to work for me as a clerk while attending college classes at night to earn his degree in economics. Boon graduated in four years and became one of my most valued employees.

It was common practice in Japan to give bonuses twice a year, one generous one at the end of the year and one lesser one in July called "Obon", a summer festival. Obon is a delightful tradition in Japan, a celebration honoring one's ancestors. It is the custom to enjoy savory snacks and put some of these treats on little boats. These boats were sent down the river to the ancestors during the day, but also at night. It was a very pretty sight to see the little boats, each holding a votive candle, floating down all sorts of waterways to revered ancestors who would enjoy the delicacies in their afterlife.

Our firm conformed to this practice. In the beginning Boon never spent any of his bonuses on himself—giving it all to his family. He had patches on his trousers and even on his shoes. Finally, I decided I would not give him money as a bonus. I started by buying him personal attire that he needed such as a pair of trousers or a pair of shoes. In later years as living standards improved, and as Boon's family started to fare better, I returned to the practice of giving monetary bonuses. For his graduation from Boon's night time university, I presented him with a tailored suit. He was so proud, no longer a boy, now he was an adult businessman.

The company started to be financially successful. Actually, we were doing better than we had done before my illness. My life took on a nice, rather comfortable routine. I enjoyed negotiating and creating new products. Coming to grips with the improbability of me ever going to the United States resulted in a kind of peace. The year of 1955 was half over and new life could be seen everywhere.

It was at this time that I received a letter from an old friend, Joe Semeraro, who had worked for the American consulate in Tokyo and had been transferred to the American consulate in Venezuela. We were good friends when he was stationed in Tokyo. In the old days, we had often gone swimming at beaches and we had climbed Mt. Fuji together, a first even for me.

It seemed one of his co-workers in the Venezuelan consulate, a young woman whose name was Lila Jacobsen, was moving to Japan to work for the U.S. Occupation Forces. She was to be stationed just outside Tokyo. Joe asked if I would take her under my wing and show her around. After her arrival, she contacted me and we went out a few times, strictly as friends. To expose her to a typical Japanese eatery, I took her to a Soba shop, which we would call a noodle soup restaurant. Purposely I chose to sit at a long free seating table. Noon is the busiest time in this kind of a place, with businessmen on the run. The very loud slurping and swallowing sounds, not considered impolite in Japan, affected her so much she could not eat. She just sat there transfixed listening to the slurping sounds of all the patrons. Proper manners sometimes change with the country.

One day, Lila, needing an escort, called and invited me to attend a party in Tokyo hosted by some members of the American consulate. No one loves parties more than I, but going to a consulate where I did not know anyone was not my idea of fun. I said yes just to be a gentleman. At the party a bunch of us were standing having drinks. One of the people standing with us happened to be a Vice-Consul. In her charming way Lila asked him "What can you do for my Chinese friend here?" pointing to me. Everyone laughed, but knew what she meant—that I was born in China. I told a short version of my life and the Vice-consul said my chances of getting into the United States on the Chinese quota were next to impossible, something, of course, I already knew. Then he asked me if I had heard of the Hungarian Refugee Relief

Act. He said it might be worth trying. I told him I was not aware of it. He then explained. Apparently, the United States had opened its doors for immigration to those refugees escaping the aftermath of the 1956 revolution in Hungary and then added many other refugees fleeing communism. The Vice-consul then told me, "If you decide to apply, you'd better hurry because all the documents have to be presented to the U.S. consulate by the end of September." It was already the middle of August.

When I arrived home that night the familiar fires of hope were reignited. Was there one more chance available to me? One could argue I was not really a refugee, but then again what was I if not a victim of communism? I decided to try once more.

I began gathering the necessary documents. This time everything went smoothly and all necessary papers were submitted before the September deadline. In regards to the necessary papers, my parents could not be my sponsors because they were not yet U.S. citizens, but they were able to ask a good friend to sponsor me. Now all I had to do was wait; something I had done most of my adult life.

∽⟔∾

In the Meantime

In late fall of that year, 1956, I got a call from another St. Joseph boy, Bill Gordes, the younger brother of my classmate, Eddie Gordes, of Tokyo Foreigners Club fame. Bill was involved with the growing Japanese entertainment industry and was a bit of an impresario. Knowing that I could make Japanese people laugh, he thought I might be a possible candidate as an emcee and entertainer for stage shows and night clubs. "It would be a terrific novelty for Japanese audiences to have a westerner who speaks Japanese like you do on stage cracking jokes", he expounded. "Why not", I said to myself. Bill arranged an audition for me before a panel of show judges. We went through some routine things, and it was decided that they would try me out. I was to be further tested by going on a three day tour in three Japanese cities outside of Tokyo. I auditioned again and to my surprise, I got the job. The plan was that a Japanese emcee and I would come on stage together, banter a bit, and introduce the other acts. The tour started and we got a lot of laughs. Wanting more, I started adlibbing. Being a novice to show business, I had no idea that was called "up-staging". My Japanese partner was a seasoned performer and didn't appreciate my encroachment. On the last night of the tour, we appeared as usual and then when we were to go on stage for the second half, my partner refused to go on. He told Bill Gordes he had had enough! Bill came over to me and said "You have to go out there alone." I went on stage solo. If that happened to me today I would have said, "No way!" and walked out. In those days I was much bolder. Maybe it was because I was in a familiar environment and I knew my audience. Who knows? To this day I do not know what I said or did. The audience kept laughing and clapping. After the show I was mobbed by the audience and even asked for my autograph!

When we finished the short, but successful tour, I was offered a full time job. The producers thought they had a star in the making. Were they kidding? Do I give up my business that I had worked so hard to develop and go into show business?

Before I could make a decision, I received a letter from the American Consulate for the final phase of obtaining entrance into the United States.

As in the past, I talked myself into being very pragmatic. If my application was denied, so be it. I had learned a long time ago that certain things happened or they didn't and you can't do a damn thing to change the outcome. I survived before and I would again. Taking chances, taking risks, going for broke, all those traits were part of me. When one is that kind of person, one has to accept the consequences—good or bad. Tough talk.

The American Consulate was located in downtown Tokyo close to the Imperial Palace in one of the impressive buildings nearby. I woke up early on the morning I was to appear at the Consulate. This was the day I would find out if my application to enter the United States would be processed or not. I showered, shaved and dressed in my best suit, white starched shirt and patterned silk tie. It was the last working day in December, 1956. I put on my winter overcoat and walked into the cold, bright day. A uniformed U.S. Marine stood at attention in front of the imposing glass doors of the Consulate. The loud flapping noise of the large American flag flying over the entrance caused me to look up. I stared at the stars and stripes for a moment and walked into the building.

I found my way to the office marked "Immigration" where I was instructed to pick up my application papers. After waiting for nearly an hour I finally heard, "Mr. Balin." I quickly stood up and accepted a large manila envelope from the aide. "Everything is in this packet. You will need one more signature from one of the immigration officers on duty." The clerk then escorted me into the adjoining office.

It was the final day for processing all applications under the Hungarian Refugee Relief Act. I looked at the man sitting behind the serviceable desk. He was middle-aged, probably in his mid-fifties, balding with thick rimmed tortoiseshell eyeglasses that had slid down on his short-bridged nose. We exchanged "Good mornings" as I sat down in a wood chair at the side of the desk handing the man the manila envelope. He took the papers out of the envelope and began scanning them one by one placing each document face down on his desk as he finished checking it. The police report, signed and approved. The sponsorship papers signed. The health report signed. Next was the application itself, the one he alone must approve and sign. He read the application, paused and seemed to be reading it over again. Putting the papers down, he looked at me and said in a brusque manner, "This says you came to Japan from Shanghai in 1947. You weren't escaping from a communist country! What made you think you qualified under the Relief Act? Why did you even apply?" he said throwing down his pen. The sound of the pen hitting the desk caused me to suck in air and not release it. I knew at that moment that this whole thing was too much of a long shot to succeed, but in my heart I had begun believing that this time I might make it.

I did not know what to say. All I could manage was, "I have waited a long time, sir. My parents and sister are there and I always believed that someday I would be allowed to join them."

"You and a thousand others!" the man said raising his voice. "Give me one good reason why you consider yourself a refugee!" he continued.

I suppose, looking back, that his annoyance and impatience was understandable. After all, he was ordered to Japan to process immigration papers for the last several months, away from his family during the holiday season. What did he care about a stateless guy who had dreamed of going to America all of his life and now knew he most likely would never get there, a guy who missed his family and was tired of not belonging anywhere.

I stood up slowly and was about to turn toward the closed door. Maybe it was anger or heartbreak that suddenly gave me the courage to speak, to try one more time. I looked down at the man and answered the question, "Sir, my mother and father were refugees. They brought me into this world as a refugee. I have lived my whole life with no nationality because of communism. I could not even claim the homeland of my parents as my own. If that doesn't make me a refugee, I don't know what would!"

I turned and started to walk toward the door. It was over. Finished. A few steps before I reached the door, I heard, "Come back."

Why was he calling me back? Probably to hand me the worthless paperwork stacked on his desk. He told me to sit down. Then I watched him while he took his pen and signed the final document that would allow me to go to America. He and I stood at the same time. He held out his hand to me, "Good luck, young man, and Happy New Year."

I was thirty-three years old.

I made all the preparations to leave Japan, arranging for my manager to run Konwal Company, severing all legal ties. I sold the family home for a good price and said my goodbyes to friends and Yoshi, who came to the airport to see me off. In late January, 1957 I flew to the United States on a Pan Am Clipper, stopping in Honolulu for three days. The day the plane landed on American soil was the happiest day of my life.

෨෪

EPILOGUE

The people that inhabit this small book of memories continued to live their lives as I did mine; some I was never to see again while others continued to be a vital part of my life. A few who were gone made second entrances.

My Parents

When my mother and father came to the United States, they settled in San Francisco, California, where my sister lived. They purchased a home a few blocks from the ocean near the famous Cliff House. Again proving to be the one who adjusted, my mother learned English and became an American citizen. My father never became proficient at any language other than Russian. Even though he may have wanted to become a citizen, I think he was afraid of failing the test and losing "face" with his wife and children. His usual response to our urging was "It can wait", in Russian, of course. My mother succumbed to emphysema at the age of seventy-two. She was a gentle woman of immeasurable strength and character.

My father spent his days fishing at a small sheltered cove called Baker's Beach, located close to the Golden Gate Bridge. Occasionally he had lunch with his Russian drinking pals. After the death of my mother, he became less active and his health began to fail. My sister and I found a suitable old age home for him. He hated it and caused women who tried to befriend him to run from him as he raised his cane shouting, "Get away from me!" Those words in Russian must have seemed very frightening to those old women. The ratio of women to men at that place was forty to two! We found another home for him and he finally, somewhat adjusted.

Because of my business requirements, I had to travel a great deal, but I visited him as often as I could. He was not in good health and had been put in the hospital for tests. I went to see him at the hospital and found him asleep, so I left. The next day, I was on my way to Carmel, a small seaside town, south of San Francisco, a favorite of tourists. My wife, who was ill with cancer, was resting there with her parents. My two young children and I were to join them for the weekend. I had a strong feeling on that Saturday morning I should see my father before leaving for Carmel.

Parking in front of the hospital, I left my kids in the car telling them I would be back in a minute. I was planning to stay only a short while as we had a long drive ahead of us. When I entered my father's hospital room, his eyes were closed, but he opened them when he heard my voice. We conversed for a short while and I said I had to leave. He cared greatly for my sick wife, and never failed to ask about her. He then pointed to his cheek, a gesture I remembered from my young boyhood. He was asking for a kiss, something he had not done for many years. I leaned over and kissed him and he closed his eyes. I left a forwarding phone number with the hospital staff, just in case. He was eighty-one years old, a man of courage, conviction and contrariness, who was Russian to the core.

When I reached Carmel, there was a message for me that he had passed away. I have often thought my father knew that it was to be the last time he would see me. That last kiss was his final, affectionate goodbye.

My Sister, Ludmila

Lala was, and still is a very attractive woman. She has an effervescent personality and loves people. When she first arrived in San Francisco she was easily able to secure a position with the Japan Travel Bureau. Some time later she was hired by a prestigious travel agency specializing in very upscale tours to Japan. The agency was owned and operated by Professor Obata, a renowned artist and an instructor at University of California, Berkley. The tours, all first class, became so popular that Professor Obata, who was getting older, asked Lala to start taking clients on her own. She balked at first, but finally accepted the challenge. Lala's tours were a huge success and literally changed her life. On her tours she met many talented and socially prominent people who became her close friends. Sometimes, after she finished a tour, she would travel to new destinations that might be suitable for her tours which now included other places besides Japan. On one of these trips, traveling in first class, she sat next to a stately, well-to-do German businessman named Heinz Cordes who traveled extensively. They eventually married and Lala moved to Germany and led a wonderful life full of travel and glamour; a life for which she was created! Heinz owned a luxury yacht and he and Lala spent many weeks a year in the Mediterranean hot spots such as Monte Carlo and Nice. Heinz passed away in 1994 of Parkinson's disease after years of devoted care by Lala. She continues to live in Hamburg and remains blond and beautiful at age eighty-four.

My High School Classmates

SERGE PETROFF lives in Mill Valley, Marin County, California, across the Golden Gate Bridge not far from where my wife and I reside. He met his attractive and athletic wife on the ski slopes of the Sierras. They fell in love, married and reared four children. Having retired from the insurance business, Serge has written and published several books on Russian history and is a respected authority on the Bolshevik Revolution. Serge has just completed a memoir of his own relating his life in Japan during the war, a very different experience to mine in Shanghai. He graduated from U.C. Berkley and is still an active and proud alumnus of that fine university.

DIMITRI VOROBIOV and I lost track of each other for many years. He was able to come to the U.S. from Japan right after the war because he had a sister here who sponsored him. He enlisted in the U.S. army where he met his wife, Anne. After serving a twenty year hitch, he went to work for the Pentagon in the intelligence department for another ten years. They raised their children and now live in Virginia, with their daughter and grandson. I visited him a few years back and saw his extensive library. On one of the shelves rested a framed picture of all four of us Russian boys at St. Joseph's with our arms around each other. None of us will ever forget those carefree days. We speak and write to each other on occasion.

BORIS OGORODNIKOV. After the war, no one had heard from Boris for many decades. Stalinist Soviet Russia was in the grip of scarcity and hardship allowing little communication with the outside world. There was a Russian family named Shapiro living in Japan during the war. There were five Shapiro sons. After the war, the parents and four of the boys immigrated to the States. The fifth brother was a leftist who went to the Soviet Union and settled in Moscow. He was a friend of Serge's younger brother and through him we found out Boris was alive and residing in Moscow.

In 1984, a few years after my wife, Yvonne, passed away, I left for a round-the-world vacation trip with my now teenage children.

While in Moscow, I tried to contact Boris in that impossible country with no phone books and almost no telephones. I called the telephone information and was told there were about twenty Boris Ogorodnikovs in Moscow. A middle name or patronym was necessary to locate anyone. No luck. It was a few more years before I returned to the U.S.S.R.

On my second trip in 1988, my cousin, Nick, from Kiev (a relative I discovered on my first trip to the U.S.S.R. in 1984) joined us in Moscow. Together we tried to locate Boris. This time, because of my having obtained Boris's patronym, which I should have remembered because it was Konstantin, we found the only Boris Konstantinovich born in China. No telephone was available, but we got his address. We decided to send a telegram. However, there were several problems. I was registered at the hotel in which we were staying, as Kon Balin. Boris did not know I had changed my name, so I signed my telegram Konstantin Balabushkin Balin. I gave him the phone number of the hotel. I asked Boris to phone after eleven P.M., because we were going to attend a ballet that night. There was no direct line to the rooms, and one had to go through the hotel operator to get connected to a guest's room. The telegram must have been a little garbled and Boris ignored it, not wanting to go out to a public phone. (This long and tedious story has the same pace as the incredibly inefficient workings of the Soviet system.) His wife, Nina, finally persuaded him to respond, having a hunch that it was somebody from the past trying to reach him. He phoned me late that night. He couldn't believe it was actually me! We arranged to have breakfast the next day. Because Boris had to work and I was leaving Moscow the next afternoon, it was the only time we could meet. When he entered the hotel, we recognized each other immediately. We were overjoyed to see each other after almost fifty years. Spontaneously, we hugged each other. The Boris I knew hadn't changed a bit. Of course, we were both no longer young men, but we were both fit and healthy and still with a full crop of hair on our heads. During breakfast, we shared our stories, happy and sad, good and bad. Before parting, Boris said he wished we could have a 50th class reunion in 1991. I replied "Why wait, why not next year"? We held the reunion in 1989, as will be mentioned later. He visited me again with his wife in 2000. Boris had outlasted the Soviet Union and could now write his own news commentaries and did so for the few years he had left. He died of cancer in 2003.

DR. LIU TAI FU - RALPH LEW— Liu Tai Fu, whom the class had known only as Ralph Lew, went to Shanghai soon after graduation and enrolled at Aurora University in the French Concession to study medicine.

The rest remained in Japan, of which, only six have survived. When I went to Shanghai, I met Ralph several times, but eventually lost track of him. I was able to track him down after the war on one of my business trips to the Orient. I met him, his wife and son in Shanghai in the mid 1980's. He had finished his medical studies and was a well respected oncologist. Doing well, at least by communist standards, he lived in a simple four storied apartment building. His apartment consisted of a sitting room, a bedroom, and simple amenities. This was considered an upper class residence. At night, in the buildings entry, there was just one low watt light bulb for four stories of steps. By European or American standards it would have been considered poor indeed. His prized possession was an electric refrigerator that was kept in his living room. The kitchen was too small to accommodate the appliance. Naturally, we talked and reminisced about our past. I was happy to see him again. He told me he was afraid of the Red Guards during the infamous Cultural Revolution because of his past and having been born in Japan. The Red Guards ruthlessly searched houses, arresting people indiscriminately. Since Ralph spoke several languages besides Chinese, he would have been a prime target. As a precaution, he had burned all his papers, documents, and foreign books, including his high school diploma.

We four Russians and our one Chinese classmate did have a class reunion in San Francisco in 1989. The three Russians in the U.S. sponsored Boris and Ralph so they could come. It was wonderful to be together after so many years. We were all at my home when the Loma Prieta earthquake hit and we liked to refer to that reunion as an earthshaking event!

Determining a Person's Heritage-- Japanese Style

Upon returning to Japan in 1947, this is what I found about the rest of our class: But before I proceed, some clarification is necessary. It should be noted that the Japanese government made a distinction between those couples who were married in a Japanese sanctioned civil ceremony and those who were married in foreign consulates. Therefore, the children born to the couples whose marriages were registered in Japan were considered Japanese citizens and subject to the military draft. When those couples whose marriages were registered in the consulates of other nations had children, their children were not citizens of Japan and therefore, could not be conscripted.

These are some examples of how this unusual system affected my friends and classmates.

EDWARD EYMARD—His father was French, his mother was Japanese and they were married in a Japanese civil ceremony. He was conscripted into the Japanese Army, served in China, returned to Yokohama and married. We saw each a few times after the war. He died in the mid 1980's of a heart attack.

HANS WOLSCHKE —His father was German, his mother was Japanese and they were married in a Japanese civil ceremony. He was conscripted into Japanese Army, served in Manchuria, taken prisoner by the Soviets, taken to Siberia and Ulan Bator, Mongolia, and returned to Tokyo at end of 1949. He married and inherited his father's meat processing business. We went night clubbing and hunting many times when I returned to Japan. Hans died of heart problem in early 1980's.

EDDIE GORDES—His father was half French and half Japanese, his mother was Japanese. Eddie was not conscripted because his parents marriage was registered with the French consulate even though he was three-quarters Japanese. After the Tokyo Foreigners Club closed, Eddie relocated to Paris, France, where he worked as an adviser and guide to Japanese businessmen and tourists. He married a French girl and had one child. I met him several times on my trips to Paris. He died of a respiratory problem in early 1990's.

DELPHINO de BRITTO—Macao Portuguese, died in a Japanese prison during the war under mysterious circumstances.

A. CHIKAMOTO— He was the Nisei who left right after graduation for Hawaii on one of the last boats that still sailed to the U.S. On my business trips to the Far East, I had to make a stop in Hawaii. I tried to track him down, with no success.

My Teachers At St. Joseph's

When the war started, there was an almost immediate exchange of enemy nationals. The American Marianist Brothers, who came to Japan because they wanted to share their love of God and there love for America with us, left for the United States. I never heard or saw any of them again. I wish I could let them know how much of my life was influenced by the friends I met and the knowledge I acquired because of their good work.

Walter (Vladimir) Goverdovsky

My good friend, Walter, was born in Tientsin, China. When things started to get really tough financially for both of us during the middle of the war years, Walter moved in with me to share the rent. It was at this time he received a letter from his sister telling him his father had been murdered. I remember he began to cry, but he never told me why or how his father was killed. In fact, he never mentioned the subject again. He ended up not graduating from St. John's and became a middle-man of sorts, a trader for buyers and sellers of everything from bicycles to booze.

After the Communist takeover of China, he, like many White Russians, was sent to the Philippines by the International Refugee Organization. From there he was able to immigrate to Australia where he became a citizen of that country. Some years after I had come to San Francisco, by chance I met a visitor from Australia who knew Walter. On one of my business trips, I was able to visit him and his wife. The handsome boy I knew had disappeared. He had gained a lot of weight, had lost most of his wavy dark hair and his relaxed stride now translated into the slow steps of an old man. It was to be the last time I saw him or heard from him. My constant remembrance of him is the "wal" in my company's name, Konwal, a name we concocted while dreaming about our future back in the 1940s.

The Russian Royals

The Baron and Baroness were rescued from their plight of poverty. They left for Paris after the war. From there they eventually were sponsored by a wealthy Russian woman living in Southern California and lived their lives as a middle class couple in Fontana, California. My parents were honored with a visit from the Baron in 1960. The Baron died in Fontana in 1962. The Baroness eventually returned to St. Petersburg and died at the age of 95 having witnessed the downfall of the hated Bolsheviks. Perhaps she was able to live out her old age as the Duchess she was born to be. What happened to the cherished treasures that I saw and held in my hands, I will never know.

The Colonel and his son, Peter, also left for Paris after the war. As far as I know, they never left France.

Ronald Kirkbride

He was quite a fellow. The year is 1959. I am now living in San Francisco, dating a girl named Yvonne Vaughan, whom I later married. She announced to me one day that she was reading a book about me. "The main character even has your last name", she said. I didn't pay much attention and accused her of exaggerating the story, as she was prone to do. "I'll bring you the book", she said defiantly.

We had a date one day to meet for lunch downtown where she was working, and when we met, she was quite distraught. "I left the book on the bus." she cried. "Oh sure", I teased. If you knew Yvonne you would know she never let me get away with anything! She searched everywhere and finally obtained a copy of the book from the publisher. Subsequently, when we met for lunch, she thrust the paperback into my hand. "Here". The book was titled "Tamiko" written by Ronald Kirkbride. What a surprise.

After Yvonne and I were married, I contacted Ronald through his publisher and Yvonne and I met him in London. He said he had tried to get in touch with me, but to no avail. He hoped I was not offended by his use of my background and name. I didn't mind, in fact, it was kind of fun. The book was made into a first run movie titled "A Girl Named Tamiko" starring British movie star, Lawrence Harvey, as Ivan Balin, Martha Hyer as the American girl and France Nuyen as Tamiko. By today's standards it is a pretty awful flick, but it was a hit in 1962.

Yoshi

The day I told Yoshi my visa was approved to enter the United States, she knew we would probably never see each other again and yet she was happy for me. She knew that it was all I ever truly wanted. Her life went on and we never completely lost touch. She met a wealthy (married) American business man who traveled regularly to the Orient. He loved Yoshi, but he would never leave his family. He helped her move to New York, and underwrote a floral arranging business for her in which she provided floral arrangements for hotels. Eventually the American man's wife passed away, and he wanted to marry Yoshi. When he told his family, they objected so strongly that the marriage never took place. Yoshi continued to do floral arrangements for hotels and started teaching Ikebana. Mike, her son, was never forgotten. It was her dream to see him again and she set her mind and energy on finding him. Find him she did. He lived in Southern California and was a policeman. His adoptive parents were very understanding and generously arranged a meeting. A strong relationship emerged between birth mother and son with the blessing of his adoptive parents.

As she aged she developed cancer that ravaged her body. We spoke on the phone several times a year and I visited her when I was in New York. She died in her New York apartment with her beloved son, Mike, at her side. He is the one who called me to say my dear friend was gone.

Sven, The Policeman

When I came to California, I heard from my father that Sven was in the Bay Area, living in San Anselmo, a small town in Marin County north of San Francisco.

I was able to contact him and was invited to his home one evening. He told me that due to his service to the allies, his permission to enter the U.S. was expedited. His brother, who was the brilliant linguist, was immediately hired as a translator for the United Nations in New York.

Sven had landed in Seattle, expecting to get a job in the field that he had proven to be proficient—law enforcement. However, much to his surprise and disappointment, he could not qualify because he was not a U.S. citizen. He left Seattle for the Bay Area, and was able to get work as a handyman at Dominican College, a Liberal Arts school for women (now a coed university). The irony of life! Here was a man, who in the past held an important position as a police officer in the French Concession of Shanghai and was a major participant in the pro-ally underground movement, and now was employed as a seemingly meek individual, wearing overalls. No one would ever have guessed that he had lived the life of a hero so many years before. Fate is not always kind. Sven and his wife later moved to Hawaii. Perhaps he got his reward after all.

Captain Hussey

After leaving Peking, the captain was transferred to Taiwan. In the meantime, he had married a beautiful Chinese widow with a very young son. One day in Tokyo, I was driving by SCAP Headquarters, when I thought I saw Capt. Hussey standing on the steps of the building. But the officer had a Major insignia, so I thought it couldn't be him, and kept on driving. I realized that he could have been promoted, and backed up, parked the car and approached him. He looked away then looked back. "Bush" he greeted me with a smile and an outstretched hand. He was visiting on official military business from Taiwan. I invited him to our house and we had dinner with my parents. That was the last I saw or heard of him.

Fumio "Boon" Tsukamoto

When I left for the States, I entrusted Boon with the management of the Konwal Trading Company and gave him part ownership. I established Konwal, San Francisco not too long after arriving in my new home. The two companies were separate entities. Once or twice a year, I went to Japan on buying trips for Konwal, S.F. and visited Boon, often staying at his house. He now had complete control of the enterprise in Japan. The typical low-end products, long associated with Japan right after the war, gradually began to change. Quality became more important than quantity. Even though Konwal, Japan had many customers, the market for the type of merchandise it handled eventually evaporated. It was decided to close down the business. Later on, Boon started his own company and did quite well. In fact, I was one of his customers. He married a beautiful, charming girl and they became the parents of twin boys. In the 1980s, I attended the elder twin's wedding in Tokyo.

Boon and I kept in touch for many years, mostly at Christmas. Sadly, I have not heard from him in the last few years. He was a very special young man.

Kon Balin

I am now eighty-six years old and in surprisingly good health. I am a proud and thankful citizen of America, the greatest country on earth. My business, Konwal Company, San Francisco allowed me to travel the world in first class accommodations for over 40 years. I sold the company in 1994 and retired. I owe a great sense of gratitude to my manager, Alan Bauer and assistant manager, Ronnie Leong, who were hard working and always loyal. I married a wonderful girl named Yvonne who was smart, funny and was of enormous help to me in life and business. We had two children who were eight and nine years old when she died of malignant melanoma, a terrible form of skin cancer. At that time I was over fifty, traveling several months of the year on business, but I tried to be a decent father to my children, but without their wonderful mother, it was most difficult. In summer we traveled extensively together and I car-pooled like every other "mother". I do not know what my children and I would have done without the loving devoted care and support we received form the Vaughans, my late wife's family. Every member of the family helped oversee the well being of the children when I traveled. I was also fortunate to have the wonderfully gentle Estella Wilkins, our African-American housekeeper, who showered the children with love and care throughout their young lives and on into their adult years. As Estella aged and became infirmed, my children, "her babies" as she always referred to them, made sure she was well cared for and showered love and attention on the woman who loved them so dearly. She recently passed away and will always be remembered most fondly.

Those years as a single father are not without regrets. I was not an easy person to deal with. It is important for me to express my sincere gratitude to those who helped me rear my children. Despite my many shortcomings my children grew up to be kind and successful adults. For that I am very grateful.

When Yvonne died, I thought about marrying again for the sake of the children, but they did not like the women I liked and I didn't particularly care for the ones they preferred, so I remained unattached until they finished high school and went on to college.

My second marriage was to a beautiful woman named Linda Stewart who was eighteen years younger than I. It was not meant to be and we were divorced after nine on-and-off years together.

At the age of 73, I was fortunate to marry an old friend, Arlene Rubens, still most attractive at age sixty. She had been a close friend of my first wife, Yvonne. Arlene, who wrote the stories you have read, was able to bring back the many feelings that were buried for a long, long time. It was not an easy task. I thank her from the bottom of my heart for her patience and insistence that this book be completed.

Having sold Konwal when I was 70, I now have the time to travel for fun. Arlene was a widow with six grown children and now seven grandchildren. We thoroughly enjoy each other and laugh a lot. I suppose my luck has continued. We've toured many exotic places in the thirteen years since we wed. It has been my pleasure to see the world again with her at my side.

As I ponder those times, I realize history always repeats itself in one way or another. Each generation must endure its share of tragedy and triumph. It is well to note by those who have similar aspirations that the incredible evil caused by the ambitious dictators of my time, who believed their empires would rule the world, are gone. Hitler, Tojo, Mussolini and Stalin are all buried. And I am still here. Amazing.

✌✌